IN
DEFENSE
OF
CAPITALISM

Newspaper Commentary
from the
Ayn Rand Institute
1996 — 2000

AYN RAND
INSTITUTE PRESS

Published by the Ayn Rand Institute Press

http://www.aynrand.org/

ISBN 0 9625336-4-5

Production by Ronen Nakash
Cover design by David Layne

Table of Contents

Introduction

In Defense of Capitalism contains a series of brief essays written under the auspices of the Ayn Rand Institute (ARI) through 1999. Most of these essays originally appeared as op-ed pieces in newspapers around the country.

ARI was established in 1985 to promote the ideas of novelist-philosopher Ayn Rand (1905–1982), best known for her novels *Atlas Shrugged* (1957) and *The Fountainhead* (1943).[1] Ayn Rand was a passionate advocate of reason, rational egoism, and individual rights. She embraced and upheld laissez-faire capitalism as the ideal economic and political social system.

In her 1966 book *Capitalism: The Unknown Ideal*, Rand defined capitalism as the "social system based on the recognition of individual rights, including property rights, in which all property is privately owned."[2] Elsewhere, she wrote: "When I say 'capitalism,' I mean a full, pure, uncontrolled, unregulated laissez-faire capitalism—with a separation of state and economics, in the same way and for the same reasons as the separation of state and church."[3]

In sharp contrast to other advocates of free markets, Ayn Rand viewed capitalism as desirable primarily because it was the only moral social system:

> The *moral* justification of capitalism does not lie in the altruist claim that it represents the best way to achieve "the common good." It is true that capitalism does—if that catch-phrase has any meaning—

but this is merely a secondary consequence. The moral justification of capitalism lies in the fact that it is the only system consonant with man's rational nature, that it protects man's survival *qua* man, and that its ruling principle is: *justice.*[4]

The essays in this book are dedicated to the defense of capitalism as the moral ideal. Rather than attempting to chronicle the innumerable attacks on capitalism and worsening encroachments on individual rights, this slim volume seeks to address a few key areas in which capitalism and capitalists are being vilified, undermined, and sabotaged.

The more ominous trends that pose a danger to capitalists include, we believe: government interference in health care issues; the environmental movement; antitrust; and multiculturalism. This is by no means an exhaustive list. But these four trends starkly illustrate the fundamental issue at stake: the need to defend free minds and free markets from those who would sacrifice your business—and your life—for the sake of the "needy," to save the "environment," to "protect" the less-able among your competitors, or to serve the cause of cultural "diversity." Sections one through four of this book deal with these four trends.

The fifth section deliberately brings together seemingly disparate issues, ranging from the commonplace (rent control) to the cutting-edge (human cloning). A close reading of these essays will, we hope, alert you to a unifying theme: that the putative "crises" we face are largely the result not of too much freedom, but of too little. This theme, in turn, reinforces the arguments already advanced in the previous four sections.

This book concludes with a series of articles celebrating achievement. Christmas, Independence Day, and Labor Day, for instance, are occasions for genuine pride in achievement. As inimical as the climate for capitalism may be today, there is still ample reason to celebrate.

In fact, to the extent that remnants of capitalism still persist in America, this itself is a cause for celebration. This is because, as Ayn Rand explained:

> Capitalism demands the very best of man—his rationality—and rewards him accordingly. It leaves every man free to choose the work he likes, to specialize in it, to trade his product for the products of others, and to go as far on the road of achievement as his ability and ambition will carry him. His success depends on the objective value of his work and on the rationality of those who recognize that value. When men are free to trade, with reason and reality as their only arbiter, when no man may use physical force to extort the consent of another, it is the best product and the best judgment that win in every field of human endeavor, and raise the standard of living—and of thought—ever higher for all those who take part in mankind's productive activity.[5]

This book is dedicated to the proposition that capitalism, as a political and economic system, is worthy both of celebration—and of a vigorous moral defense.

Yaron Brook
President and Executive Director
Ayn Rand Institute

References

1. A brief biography of Ayn Rand and more information about ARI appear at the end of this book.
2. Ayn Rand, "What Is Capitalism?" in *Capitalism: The Unknown Ideal* (New York: Penguin Books, 1966), p. 19.
3. Ayn Rand, "The Objectivist Ethics," in *The Virtue of Selfishness* (New York: Penguin Books, 1964), p. 33.
4. "What Is Capitalism?" p. 20.
5. Ayn Rand, "For the New Intellectual," in *For the New Intellectual* (New York: Penguin Books, 1961), p. 24.

Section I:
Man's Life

> *[The capitalist] is the great liberator, who in the short span of a century and a half has released men from bondage to their physical needs, has released them from the terrible drudgery of an eighteen-hour workday of manual labor for their barest subsistence, has released them from famines, from pestilences, from the stagnant hopelessness and terror in which most of mankind had lived in all the pre-capitalist centuries and in which most of it still lives today in non-capitalistic countries.*

—Ayn Rand, "For the New Intellectual,"
For the New Intellectual (1961), pg. 26.

Despite the overwhelming evidence that supports the observation above, critics ignore the astonishing accomplishments of science, technology, and capitalists and focus on alleged shortcomings—often utterly contrived—as evidence that the "free market" is failing and that government remedies are called for.

Over the past few years, for example, much has been written about the "crisis" in health care. Amazingly, pundits and politicians alike point to the "free market" as the villain. Inadequate government involvement in health care, it is argued, results in care that is too expensive, inefficient, and "unfair" in its exclusion of millions of individuals.

These critics call for varying degrees of increased government regulation of the health care sector as the only means to achieve affordable and "fair" coverage for all. Further, these individuals argue for increased regulation of personal decisions (e.g., smoking).

As these essays argue, the free market is not the source of the crisis in health care—but rather the cure. The astonishing rise in life expectancy and quality of life, as well as advances in medical technology, has been achieved in spite of, rather than due to, government interference in the health care industry and "public health" issues.

Attacking the Heart of Medicine

by Richard M. Salsman

One vital fact was omitted in the news accounts about the success of Boris Yeltsin's recent heart surgery: the failure of socialized medicine. And this fact underscores the question of whether America's health care policies are courting a similar failure.

Competent physicians with specialized technical skills are scarce in Russia. Yeltsin, because of his privileged position, had access to qualified cardiologists—an access unavailable to most Russians. And even Yeltsin's doctors had to rely heavily on the training and advice of American heart specialists. For example, Dr. Renet Akchurin, the head surgeon on the Yeltsin operation, was trained by an American pioneer in the field, Michael DeBakey. While DeBakey did not apply the scalpel to Yeltsin, he was called on to make the crucial decisions not only about the diagnosis but about the timing and the method of Yeltsin's surgery.

But the rest of the country has virtually no modern health care. Bypass operations, now routine in the United States (300,000 per year), remain rare in Russia (3,000 per year). Most are done by American-trained doctors at special facilities reserved for political leaders. Heart surgery is "free" for Russian citizens, but 98 percent of those needing bypass operations die without getting them. Patients suffer and die on interminable waiting lists. Some choose not to even seek needed care. Dr.

Yevgeny Rogozin, of Moscow's Cardiology Center, reveals that "Many people in this country are afraid to let someone take a knife to their heart." What they fear are the scalpels wielded by socialists.

Why is this so? Because decades of socialism have replaced conscientious medical professionals with low-skilled, mindless bureaucrats. Scrupulous rationality and independent thinking are the key traits of a good doctor. But these are the very traits penalized, and then destroyed, by socialism. Under socialism, doctors have no freedom to choose the terms under which they work: not whom they treat, nor how, nor at what price. They must surrender their private concerns and serve the "public interest." There is no profit in being a good Russian doctor—so good doctors disappear. Patients are thus left in the incompetent hands of those who are skilled—not in advanced medical procedures—but in obedience to government directives.

In medicine, as in other fields, the socialists must turn to the capitalists for help. American medicine has been the envy of the world, because at its heart stands the independent doctor, left free to think and act by the standard of his own rational self-interest. His judgment is not subordinated to the dictates of government bureaucrats.

But freedom is now under attack. *Capitalist doctors are being replaced by medical bureaucrats*—and medical care in America is slowly vanishing. When Medicare and Medicaid subsidies were initiated in the 1960s, it was claimed that doctors would retain their freedom. But when government foots the bill, it first inflates costs, then realizes it must control the spending of the "public's" money. In order to cap skyrocketing costs, the government now herds doctors and patients into HMOs, where care is rationed. Doctors are under "gag orders" not to alert patients to alternative, life-saving—but costly—procedures.

HMOs are increasingly staffed by generalists, and medical specialization is declining—a big step down the socialist road to medical incompetence and barbarism. Tragically, the results of this socialization of medicine—rationing and deteriorating care—are now blamed on private doctors and the profit motive.

Even as it deteriorates, American medical care is being made compulsory. The Kennedy-Kassenbaum bill, for instance, imposes fines and prison terms on doctors who fail to comply with regulations governing subsidized tests and treatments. Many conscientious doctors are quitting. The capitalist doctor—independent, expert, caring—is an endangered species.

Dr. Thomas Hendricks, the brain surgeon in Ayn Rand's 1957 novel, *Atlas Shrugged,* who flees from socialist medicine, explains his choice as follows:

> I have often wondered at the smugness with which people assert their right to enslave me, to control my work, to force my will, to violate my conscience, to stifle my mind—yet what is it that they expect to depend on, when they lie on an operating table under my hands? Let them discover the kind of doctors that their system will now produce. Let them discover, in their operating rooms and hospital wards, that it is not safe to place their lives in the hands of a man whose life they have throttled. It is not safe, if he is the sort

of man who resents it—and still less safe, if he is the sort who doesn't.

Americans will see more and more of this sort of doctor—unless we categorically reject government involvement in medicine.

Clinton vs. Your Health

by Richard E. Ralston

In 1994 President Clinton proposed a national health care plan with a central pillar of forcing more Americans into HMOs. His ultimate objective was the complete government takeover of all health care.

But the Clinton administration has now discovered that HMOs are not so wonderful, which most of us knew all along. The President is now advocating legislation which will require HMOs to provide patients with a wide range of additional services as a "right," but at no additional cost to the patients. But Clinton can't succeed in making a legal requirement out of a metaphysical impossibility. Good health cannot be legislated. There will be costs to the patients: the destruction of the medical profession and of individual health. When your health falls apart or you die, you will now be able to bring suit against the HMO for failing to perform the impossible. (This legislation therefore may at least improve the incomes of the members of the Trial Lawyers Association.)

America had the best health care system in the world until the government began to mandate that various groups had "rights" to unlimited health care whatever the cost. This resulted in an explosion in costs and rationing of health care. The government response has always been: more mandated care, more spending, more rationing, more controls. The free market system provided the best health care to the most people at the lowest cost. Were it allowed to operate, it could do so again. In such a free market, you would be free to make all of your own health care decisions and to make provision for the cost of your health care through insurance or savings. But the last thing the Clinton administration wants is for people to manage their own health care. They want *everyone* to depend on government for their health care.

The desire to make people dependent on government underlies a wide variety of programs which control all aspects of your daily life. These programs are based on malicious ideas which the government hopes that you will accept unchallenged—so they can shove the programs down your throat. For example: If you act to take care of your *own* health needs and obtain insurance, you first have to pay tax on the money you need for premiums. The Clinton administration opposes any tax relief for those who save for their own health care needs through medical savings accounts (MSAs), because it would undercut "the system," which provides for those who do not have insurance or savings. The political premise is: better that no one have good health care if someone, somewhere, does not have it. It is the same political premise that opposes a voucher system to break up the government monopoly on education because it would undercut "the system," which provides education for the poor. Better that every young person be subjected to a wretched bureaucracy that educates no one, than to allow most parents to find a decent education for their own children. Better that misery be spread equally than to allow you to provide for your own health care and the education of your own children. These beliefs are based on the false moral premise that it is evil for you to manage your own affairs and live a happy life if somebody, somewhere, is unhappy.

Is government takeover of medicine facing any significant opposition? Not from the Republicans, the supposed defenders of the free market. Typically, they are racing each other to propose legislation which will do only slightly less damage than Clinton to a free market for health care. Only a few redeeming features of the Republican proposals have merit, such as permanently allowing for more medical savings accounts, or once again allowing elderly patients to pay with their own money for procedures not covered by Medicare.

If you want a return to high quality, affordable health care, tell Congress you do not want more government control of HMOs, that you do not want HMOs at all, and that the government should get out of health care completely. Demand the right to choose your own health care, the chance to buy health insurance free of taxation, and the freedom to save for your own health care needs in a tax-free medical savings account.

Graduated Tax for Medicare Is Immoral

by Arthur Mode, M.D.

The U.S. Congress has been considering a steep increase in Medicare taxes for higher-income people. A tax that has been flat since its inception in the 1960s is suddenly about to become a graduated tax. If the measure becomes law, the tax for higher-income earners will jump from about $500 annually to more than $2,000.

Lawmakers pushing for the increase have faced no moral opposition. These lawmakers have actually claimed the moral high ground, pressing the tired, old claim that individuals with higher incomes can afford the higher tax rates. The opposing principle, that all individuals should be treated equally under the law, has not been brought into the sunlight, not by any Congressman, not by media commentators, and not by the proposed victims—the wealthier taxpayers—who have been virtually silent as their fleecing looms near.

In the absence of principled opposition, the measure will pass. There is no vocal principled opposition to it because no one has challenged the definition of "fairness" implicit in the legislation, namely, that it is fair that people with higher incomes have fewer rights and, therefore, should be compelled to pay more because they have a greater "ability to pay." The American people do not usually oppose measures they perceive as fair. As a general rule: in an argument or debate, whoever controls the definition of what is moral will win. Unfortunately,

Unfortunately, the "ability to pay" principle has controlled the debate in the area of tax law.

Most Americans accept the idea that if two men commit the same crime, they should receive the same punishment. Equal treatment under the law for criminal offenses is considered just. If a Congressman were to propose that, for the same offense, Hispanics should be given longer jail terms, or that Catholics should never be subjected to capital punishment, he would be hooted down.

When the subject changes from criminal to tax law, the concept of equal treatment under the law suddenly goes halfway out the window. Halfway, because there would be no support for taxing *some* groups differentially, e.g., higher rates for certain religious groups, racial groups, or genders. Such unequal treatment is still viewed as wrong. But equal treatment *does* go out the window when one group is mentioned: the rich.

Why the silent acquiescence to this one exception? Is it because the "ability to pay" proponents have some sparkling new argument that crushes all opposition? Not at all. Their position is based on stale Marxist class-envy politics. Karl Marx and Friedrich Engels were so eager to destroy the successful upper- and middle-class "bourgeoisie" that they advocated a heavy graduated income tax in their *Communist Manifesto* in 1848. The notion that the wealth and income of the rich could be forcibly redistributed in the form of government benefits and handouts to lower-income people appealed to the worst elements then, and that is just as true today. Socialist and populist politicians have all played upon this envy. The more able, enterprising, and successful citizens have been repeatedly set up for tax attacks. Ayn Rand identified the motive of such attacks: hatred of people who possess virtues or talents (including the talent for making money) the envy-ridden regard as desirable but do not themselves possess. Or, in Ayn Rand's words, "hatred of the good for being the good."

Over the years, many decent Americans have either forgotten or become careless about consistently applying the principle of equal treatment under all laws, not just criminal laws. More Americans can recite the Marxist line: "From each according to his ability, to each according to his needs," than can remember these words by John Adams, one of our Founding Fathers: "It must be remembered, that the rich are people as well as the poor; that they have rights as well as others; that they have as clear and as sacred a right to their large property as others have to theirs which is smaller; that oppression to them is as possible and as wicked as to others."

The important question is whether enough Americans have the clear-headed courage to face down the socialists and populists to regain control of the definition of "fairness," and reinstate its crucial moral principle: equal treatment under every law in America.

Patient "Bill of Rights": An Assault on Rights

by Robert W. Tracinski

To deal with the problems in health care, the House of Representatives passed a dangerous measure supposedly guaranteeing patients a bill of rights. This is a sham, because this bill actually would diminish the freedom of doctors, hospitals, insurance companies—and the very patients it purports to protect.

The bill is an attempt to grant special privileges to some—to be paid for by trampling on the rights of others. It decrees, for example, that health insurance must provide certain benefits, such as longer hospital stays and coverage for a wider variety of treatments.

But these mandated benefits are not free; someone has to pay for them. Will insurance companies be forced to absorb the extra spending on these benefits? Or will the expense be shared by doctors and hospitals, who will be paid less for their work? Or will the cost be passed on to patients, who will have to pay higher premiums for health insurance, making it too expensive for some of them to afford? The one certainty is that *someone* will be forced to foot the bill to provide the care mandated by Congress. When it comes to all these "someones"—where is the concern for *their* rights?

Genuine rights—the kind protected by the original Bill of Rights—guarantee the individual's freedom of action, including the act of trading with others, without being subject to government coercion. But the pseudo-rights being peddled today are actually *violations* of rights. They are attempts to dole out special government favors, to be given to some by taking away the freedom of others. They are attempts to force people—the people whose abilities have made these medical services possible—to provide their services on terms they would not voluntarily accept.

In fact, this anti-rights approach is exactly what has caused the very problems a patients' "Bill of Rights" pretends to solve. When Medicare was passed in 1965, politicians promised that it would provide the elderly with a "right to health care." But once health care was "free"—i.e., paid for by someone else—patients (and doctors) had little incentive to control costs. The result was an ever-rising bill for taxpayers. Where was the concern for *their* rights?

In the '70s and '80s, the government "solved" the problem of escalating costs by imposing comprehensive price controls on doctors and hospitals—while still requiring them to provide exactly the same services. Where was the concern for *their* rights? In response to this squeeze, health care providers shifted the costs to private customers, leading to skyrocketing costs for anyone under 65. Where was the concern for *their* rights?

Rising prices led to rising insurance premiums, and in an attempt to provide affordable coverage, insurers began to institute "managed care" systems. These became notorious for cutting costs by sacrificing quality. As a result of government intervention, the normal free-market link between offering a quality product and enjoying financial success was severed. Instead, in medicine, the worse the service, the better were the profits. While every industry in which the free market prevailed experienced falling prices and ever-improving products—computers are just one obvious example—the opposite took place in medicine. Prices rose while service was cut.

Congress now proposes to address this problem—a problem caused by the government's systematic contempt for rights—by passing a "Patients' Bill of Rights" that would expand this assault on rights. It generated this crisis by granting special privileges to some at the expense of others—and somehow seeks to solve it by granting even more privileges and further violating the rights of those who are expected to pay for it all.

Washington has created a statist system under which there is a perpetual conflict of interest among all the participants in medical care. We do not have such conflicts between buyers and sellers of, say, bread or shoes or homeowners insurance. It is only government controls that have made medicine such a conflict-laden, bureaucrat-driven field.

We can only begin to reverse the damage by upholding genuine rights—the individual right of both patients and health care providers to be free from government interference. If our politicians really want to fight for rights, let them fight for a free market in medicine.

The Tobacco Gestapo

by David Harriman

The settlement between the tobacco industry and the government describes the new arrangement as an "historic change." That much is true—but not in the sense the drafters intended. This settlement represents a frightening, unprecedented violation of individual rights.

Under its proposed terms, the government will become the de facto owner of all the tobacco companies; the nominal owners will just follow Washington's orders, as their property is effectively expropriated. Consider, for instance, the regulations on advertising and marketing.

All print ads will be censored for content, and the use of figures such as the Marlboro Man and Joe Camel will be outlawed. The industry will be prevented from publicly issuing its views on scientific or medical aspects of smoking. The state will additionally forbid tobacco companies from using outdoor advertising, sponsoring public events, imprinting their logos on non-tobacco products (such as T-shirts), or employing any color other than black in their print ads. Not satisfied with such despotic controls over a product people voluntarily purchase, the government will also force the companies *to pay for ads condemning their own products and urging the public not to buy them.*

Has the First Amendment been abolished, you ask? Conceding that the companies' freedom of speech will be violated, the government has gotten them to "consent"—under threat of further extortion—to waive their constitutional rights.

Imagine the flood of protests the liberals would launch if the victim were, say, an accused serial killer. Yet, because the target is Big Business, they readily endorse such authoritarian measures.

What about the individual's right to his property—the right of sellers and buyers to freely deal with one another? There is, after all, no fraud involved with selling cigarettes. Everyone knows there are health risks associated with smoking. Why is the state denying the individual's freedom to make his own choices and bear responsibility for the consequences?

This campaign is a witch hunt, in which the tobacco industry is being punished for every individual's decision to smoke. (And, in a ludicrous extension of this injustice, the industry will be fined billions of dollars if teenage smoking does not decline by some arbitrarily fixed quota.)

The tobacco settlement is more dangerous than an outright prohibition of cigarettes, in that it establishes a precedent for totalitarian control over legally functioning businesses. There is a name for a system that retains the facade of private ownership while delivering actual control over people's lives to the state: *fascism*. This form of tyranny characterizes all fascist regimes in history. But in America, instead of some racial or religious minority, the unpopular minority selected as whipping boy is Big Business.

Politicians of the right and left claim that this fascist takeover of the tobacco industry promotes the "public good." This means that we as individuals are not to be permitted to make our own choices, but that government must decide what is good for us and force us to live accordingly. Well, that is the traditional argument of all dictatorships—one that certainly represents an "historic change" in the country once called "the land of the free."

If our government can justify this, what can it *not* justify? Any business offering a product that can be used, or misused, in any way that conceivably threatens the "public good" is now a candidate for state takeover. Why shouldn't government regulate sunbathing and outlaw ads for beach resorts, on the grounds that sunlight can cause skin cancer? Why shouldn't Washington tell us what to eat, how to dress, and when to exercise? Why shouldn't bureaucrats—in order to protect us against ideas incompatible with the "public good"—dictate the content of books, movies, and television shows (this last is in fact already in progress)?

Liberty is an empty concept if we are not free to make these choices for ourselves—even mistaken choices that may turn out to be harmful.

Our government has made smoking into a battleground for freedom. If we allow it to outlaw the Marlboro Man, we are paving the way for another symbol to take his place: the swastika.

Clearly, most Americans don't realize what is at stake. But anyone who values individual rights should unequivocally denounce this massive expansion of government power. It makes no difference whether you smoke or not. The fundamental issue is whether you are free to live as you choose, or are forced to live as the state commands.

Section II:
Man's Environment

If you consider, not merely the length, but the kind of life men have to lead in the undeveloped parts of the world—"the quality of life," to borrow, with full meaning, the ecologists' meaningless catch phrase—if you consider the squalor, the misery, the helplessness, the fear, the unspeakably hard labor, the festering diseases, the plagues, the starvation, you will begin to appreciate the role of technology in man's existence. Make no mistake about it: it is technology and progress that the nature-lovers are out to destroy.

—Ayn Rand, "The Anti-Industrial Revolution,"
Return of the Primitive (1999), p. 279.

Radical environmentalists are on the march—launching a full-scale attack on science, technology, and business.

The fundamental flaw in the environmentalist philosophy is that it elevates "the environment" over people. The environment is a "value," they assert. But a value to whom, and for what purpose?

Ayn Rand maintained that a *value* cannot exist independent of a *valuer*. And that valuer is man. The environment's only true value is its value in sustaining and serving man's life; our very survival depends on changing and shaping nature to further human life.

The following essays demonstrate that the core of

the environmentalist philosophy is not a reverence for nature, but rather a disregard—if not outright hatred—for mankind.

Man vs. Nature

by Peter Schwartz

For the first time in American history, the government is ordering the destruction of a dam—for environmental reasons.

This July [1999], Edwards Dam, a small hydroelectric facility on the Kennebec River in Augusta, Maine, will be torn down by the Federal Energy Regulatory Commission. Its crime? It is blocking the path of fish that swim upstream to spawn. As recounted in a *New York Times* article, "the hindrance the Edwards Dam posed to migratory fish outweighed the benefit it provided in electric generation."

On Earth Day, it is worth noting this event, for it illuminates the essential meaning of environmentalism. The closing of Edwards Dam is the implementation of environmentalism's fundamental, though often unrecognized, tenet: that man ought to be sacrificed for the sake of nature.

The common view of environmentalism is that its goal is the betterment of mankind—that it wants to purify our air and clean up our parks so that we can live healthier and happier lives. But that is a very superficial interpretation. When environmentalists are faced with a conflict between the "interests" of nature and those of man, it is man who is invariably sacrificed. If there is a choice between electric power for human beings and swimming lanes for salmon, it is always the fish that are given priority. If there is a choice between cutting down trees for human use and leaving them untouched for the spotted owl, it is always the bird's home that is saved and human habitation that goes unbuilt. Why?

Because the requirements of human life are not the standard by which environmentalists make their judgments. Their goal is to maintain nature in its virginal state—despite the demonstrable harm this inflicts upon people. They want to preserve wildernesses, to enshrine wetlands, to tear down dams and levees—i.e., to prevent the man-made "intrusions" upon nature.

In the case of Edwards Dam, for instance, they want to protect the salmon not because it is a source of food—or of any other human value. (They regularly denounce hatcheries as "unnatural" and commercial fishing as the "exploitation of nature"—and the very eating of animals as insensitive "speciesism.") Rather, they regard the "welfare" of the salmon as an end in itself—for the sake of which man must forgo the benefits of the dam.

Environmentalists often declare their philosophy openly. For example, David Graber, an environmentalist with the National Parks Service, described himself as among those who "value wilderness for its own sake, not for what value it confers upon mankind. . . . We are not interested in the utility of a particular species, of free-flowing river, or ecosystem to mankind. They have intrinsic value, more value—to me—than another human body, or a billion of them."

David Foreman, founder of the organization Earth First, bluntly stresses the environmental irrelevance of human beings: "Wilderness has a right to exist for its own sake, and for the sake of the diversity of the life forms it shelters; we shouldn't have to justify the existence of a wilderness area by saying: 'Well, it protects the watershed, and it's a nice place to backpack and hunt, and it's pretty.'"

The environmentalist goal, in other words, is to protect nature, not for man, but from man.

But this means that man must suffer so that nature remains pristine. Human beings survive by reshaping nature to fulfill their needs. Every single step taken to advance beyond the cave—every rock fashioned into a tool, every square foot of barren earth made into productive cropland, every drop of crude petroleum transformed into fuel for cars and planes—constitutes an improvement in human life, achieved by altering our natural environment. The environmentalists' demand that nature be protected against human "encroachments" means, therefore, that man must be sacrificed in order to preserve nature. If "wilderness has a right to exist for its own sake"—then man does not.

Litter-free streets or pollution-free air—or any provable benefit to man—is not what environmentalists seek. Their aim is to eliminate the benefits of the man-made in order to preserve—unchanged—nature's animals, plants, and dirt.

Earth Day is an appropriate occasion for challenging the environmentalists' philosophy. It can be the occasion for recognizing the Earth as a value—not in and of itself, but only insofar as it is continually reshaped by man to serve his ends.

On Earth Day, Remember: If Environmentalists Succeed, They Will Make Human Life Impossible

by Michael S. Berliner

Earth Day approaches, and with it a grave danger faces mankind. The danger is not from acid rain, global warming, smog, or the logging of rain forests, as environmentalists would have us believe. The danger to mankind is from environmentalism.

The fundamental goal of environmentalists is not clean air and clean water; rather it is the demolition of technological/industrial civilization. Their goal is not the advancement of human health, human happiness, and human life; rather it is a subhuman world where "nature" is worshipped like the totem of some primitive religion.

In a nation founded on the pioneer spirit, environmentalists have made "development" an evil word. They inhibit or prohibit the development of Alaskan oil, offshore drilling, nuclear power—and every *other* practical form of energy. Housing, commerce, and jobs are sacrificed to spotted owls and snail darters. Medical research is sacrificed to the "rights" of mice. Logging is sacrificed to the "rights" of trees. No instance of the progress which brought man out of the cave is safe from the onslaught of those "protecting" the environment from man, whom they consider a rapist and despoiler by his very essence.

Nature, they insist, has "intrinsic value," to be revered for its own sake, irrespective of any benefit to man. As a consequence, man is to be prohibited from using nature for his own ends. Since nature supposedly has value and goodness in itself, any human action which changes the environment is necessarily immoral. Of course, environmentalists invoke the doctrine of intrinsic value not against wolves that eat sheep or beavers that gnaw trees; they invoke it only against man, only when *man* wants something.

The ideal world of environmentalists is not 20th-century Western civilization; it is the Garden of Eden, a world with no human intervention in nature, a world without innovation or change, a world without effort, a world where survival is somehow guaranteed, a world where man has mystically merged with the "environment." Had the environmentalist mentality prevailed in the 18th and 19th centuries, we would have had no Industrial Revolution, a situation environmentalists would cheer—at least those few who might have managed to survive without the life-saving benefits of modern science and technology.

The expressed goal of environmentalism is to prevent man from changing his environment, from intruding on nature. That is why environmentalism is fundamentally anti-man. Intrusion is necessary for human survival. Only by intrusion can man avoid pestilence and famine. Only by intrusion can man control his life and project long-range goals. Intrusion improves the environment, if by "environment" one means the surroundings of man—the external material conditions of human life. Intrusion is a requirement of human nature. But in the environmentalists' paean to "Nature," *human* nature is omitted. For the environmentalists, the "natural" world is a world without man. Man has no legitimate needs, but trees, ponds, and bacteria somehow do.

They don't mean it? Heed the words of the consistent environmentalists. "The ending of the human epoch on Earth," writes philosopher Paul Taylor in *Respect for Nature: A Theory of Environmental Ethics*, "would most likely be greeted with a hearty 'Good riddance!'" In a glowing review of Bill McKibben's *The End of Nature*, biologist David M. Graber writes (*Los Angeles Times*, October 29, 1989): "Human happiness [is] not as important as a wild and healthy planet....Until such time as Homo Sapiens should decide to rejoin nature, some of us can only hope for the right virus to come along." Such is the naked essence of environmentalism: it mourns the death of one whale or tree but actually welcomes the death of billions of people. A more malevolent, man-hating philosophy is unimaginable.

The guiding principle of environmentalism is self-sacrifice, the sacrifice of longer lives, healthier lives, more prosperous lives, more enjoyable lives, i.e., the sacrifice of human lives. But an individual is not born in servitude. He has a moral right to live his own life for his own sake. He has no duty to sacrifice it to the needs of others and certainly not to the "needs" of the non-human.

To save mankind from environmentalism, what's needed is not the appeasing, compromising approach of those who urge a "balance" between the needs of man and the "needs" of the environment. To save mankind requires the wholesale rejection of environmentalism as hatred of science, technology, progress, and human life. To save mankind requires the return to a philosophy of reason and individualism, a philosophy which makes life on earth possible.

The "Green" Unabomber

by Robert W. Tracinski

As Ted Kaczynski goes on trial for the terrorist attacks attributed to the Unabomber, many are lamenting the bad press he has brought to the environmentalist movement. How unfortunate, the general sentiment goes, that the actions of one lone madman should tarnish such an admirable cause. He is not one of us, environmentalists adamantly declare.

Isn't he?

In the cause of preserving "wild nature," the Unabomber, in his "manifesto," calls for a "revolution against the industrial system." He acknowledges that, as a result, "many people will die" because the world's population "cannot even feed itself . . . without advanced technology." But such deaths must be accepted "stoically," he notes, because they are "part of the nature of things." It is urgent to preserve an untouched nature, the Unabomber asserts, even if the effects on human life are disastrous.

Is this philosophy different *in principle* from the views of mainstream environmentalists? Is this different from the elevation of the "welfare" of the snail darter and the spotted owl above the welfare of man? Isn't the Unabomber adopting the environmentalists' objective of defending nature by restricting industry and technology? Leaving aside, for the moment, the question of the Unabomber's methods, isn't his basic goal—his fundamental value—identical to that of environmentalists?

When a drug called taxol, found in the bark of the Yew tree, was discovered to be an effective treatment for breast and ovarian cancer, environmentalists blocked large-scale harvesting in order to save the forests. What about the people dying of cancer?

Nature, they said, has priority.

When the man-made pesticide DDT was still being used, malaria (which is carried by mosquitoes) was almost eradicated worldwide. Today, with the environmentalists having lobbied to ban DDT, a resurgence of malaria is killing about five million people every year. Yet, while the alleged effects of DDT on birds generated horrified outrage on the part of environmentalists, the incontestable destruction of human life caused by the *absence* of DDT generates only indifference.

These are not isolated instances. In case after case— whether it is the irradiation of food to kill deadly bacteria, the construction of dams to provide clean water and electricity, or the clearing of bug-infested swampland to make room for houses and shopping malls—the environmentalists consistently oppose industrial and technological development. They oppose it—and are willing to pay the price in human misery and deaths.

Mainstream environmentalists proclaim that the preservation of nature ought to be valued above human interests. Well, the Unabomber is merely taking that idea seriously. As the noted environmentalist Kirkpatrick Sale has said: "The problem is that technology is overwhelming us psychologically, economically, socially. I think that has to be on the agenda and talked about. And I think that's exactly what the Unabomber succeeded in doing."

According to one of the defense lawyers in the World Trade Center bombing case, the mass media "presented [Kaczynski] as a pop hero, a rebel who was protesting the encroaching oppression of technology." Given the premise that technology is oppressive, he *is* a "pop hero." The Unabomber embraces the essential tenet of environmentalism—the tenet that the man-made is abhorrent, that the "natural" is noble, and thus that man must be sacrificed to nature.

Now, most environmentalists ostensibly condemn the Unabomber. They say that the Unabomber's *methods* are antithetical to theirs. They insist that they do not support the killing of people in pursuit of environmental goals.

But don't they?

Does it matter to the woman dying of cancer that the man standing in the way of a cure is not a mad bomber, but a lawyer for the Audubon Society? Does it matter to the African father whose child has died from malaria that the death was caused, not by a terrorist, but by a bureaucrat following legal procedures?

As the effects of environmentalism become more evident—when food rots in the homes of those who lack refrigeration (because CFCs have been banned and the alternatives are too costly), when houses are unheated (because the use of fossil fuels has been curtailed), when farmers cannot grow enough food (because chemical fertilizers and pesticides have been prohibited), when we are denied life-saving new medicines (because genetic engineering has been outlawed)—will we be better off because it was done by legislation rather than terrorism?

Kaczynski's prosecutors have argued that they should be allowed to ask for the death penalty because the Unabomber's writings show a "hatred of people." It is time to ask whether the same accusation can be leveled against the environmentalist movement as a whole.

Man: The Endangered Species

by Glenn Woiceshyn

An eco-terrorist group called Earth Liberation Front (ELF) claimed responsibility for recently incinerating four ski lifts and three buildings worth $12 million—America's worst act of eco-terrorism in terms of property damage—on a mountain at Vail, Colorado. Vail's plans to expand its ski area apparently clashed with environmentalists' plans to re-introduce the lynx into Colorado. ELF arsonists claimed they torched Vail property "on behalf of the lynx" and warned skiers to ski elsewhere this winter.

While "mainstream" environmental groups may try to distance themselves from ELF and its terrorist methods, the truth is that ELF did on its own what "mainstream" environmentalists have been doing for years via the U.S. government's Endangered Species Act (ESA).

Since becoming law in 1973, the ESA has been used in countless ways to inflict harm on people in the name of protecting endangered species and their habitats. The Northern Spotted Owl became famous when timber production was virtually halted in the Pacific Northwest to protect the species. In Oregon in 1992, the water regularly supplied to several Oregon farmers from the Klamath Irrigation Project near the Oregon-California border was cut off by government to protect the shortnose sucker and the Lost River sucker, causing severe damages to crops and livestock.

In California, construction was halted on the San Bernardino Medical Center and, later, on a neighboring subdivision to protect the Delhi Sands flower-loving fly. Near Bakersfield, California, a farmer was arrested in 1994 by Fish and Wildlife officers for inadvertently killing five Tipton kangaroo rats while plowing his own soil. His tractor and plow were seized as "murder weapons." Under the ESA he faced heavy fines and three years in prison.

Whenever man's needs conflict with the "interests of nature," environmentalists take the side of nature.

The real motive behind environmentalism is stated by David Graber (a biologist with the U.S. National Park Service): "We are not interested in the utility of a particular species, or free-flowing river, or ecosystem to mankind. They have intrinsic value, more value—to me—than another human body, or a billion of them." This "intrinsic value" ethic means that man must value nature—not for any benefit to man, but because nature is somehow a value in and of itself. Hence, nature must be kept pristine despite the harm this causes man. We must halt activities beneficial to us, such as farming, forestry, and treatment of cancer, in order to safeguard fish, birds, trees, and rats.

Throughout history, people were told to sacrifice their lives to God, the community, the state, or the Fuehrer—all with deadly consequences. Now we are being told to sacrifice our lives to nature. And current environmental legislation, such as the ESA, provides government with massive powers to enforce such sacrifices. What disasters could such power lead to?

Some environmentalists have expressed their preference. "Until such time as Homo sapiens should decide to rejoin nature," writes biologist Graber, "some of us can only hope for the right virus to come along." City University of New York philosophy Professor Paul Taylor adds: "[T]he ending of the human epoch on Earth would most likely be greeted with a hearty 'Good Riddance!'"

While extreme, these anti-human sentiments are logically consistent with environmentalism's "intrinsic value" philosophy: Since man survives only by conquering nature, man is an inherent threat to the "intrinsic value" of nature and must therefore be eliminated. Environmentalism makes man the endangered species.

The only antidote to these haters of mankind and their anti-human philosophy is to uphold man's right to pursue his own life. His nature demands that he does this best by improving his environment through technology, production, and development.

Because governments are supposed to protect individual rights, not violate them, we should stop handing government the power to sacrifice people to nature and demand that it relinquish any such power it currently wields. One obvious place to start is for Congress to abolish the Endangered Species Act, not just "reform" it as some Republicans are trying to do.

As for the eco-terrorists who destroy property and (in the case of the Unabomber) even maim or kill people, they would not be so brazen in expressing their hatred for man through terrorism were in not for the moral sanction they currently derive from the anti-human philosophy underlying environmentalism. Furthermore, government properly stripped of its power to sacrifice people to nature would have more resources and re-solve to track these terrorists down and bring them to justice.

Section III:
Hatred of the Good

The antitrust laws—an unenforceable, uncompliable, unjudicable mess of contradictions—have for decades kept American businessmen under a silent, growing reign of terror. . . . Under the antitrust laws, a man becomes a criminal from the moment he goes into business, no matter what he does. For instance, if he charges prices which some bureaucrats judge as too high, he can be prosecuted for monopoly or for a successful 'attempt to monopolize'; if he charges prices lower than those of his competitors, he can be prosecuted for 'unfair competition' or 'restraint of trade'; and if he charges the same prices as his competitors, he can be prosecuted for 'collusion' or 'conspiracy.' There is only one difference in the legal treatment accorded to a criminal or to a businessman: the criminal's rights are protected much more securely and objectively than the businessman's.

—Ayn Rand, "Choose Your Issues,"
The Objectivist Newsletter (January 1962), p. 1.

As of this writing, the U.S. Department of Justice is seeking radical "legal remedies" that may entail the breakup and/or severe regulation of Microsoft Corporation. While many of the essays in this section deal specifically with this high-profile event, the issues at stake are far larger than the immediate fate of one company.

Whatever the ultimate outcome of the Microsoft trial, there is an enduring principle underlying this case. Antitrust laws—dating back to Standard Oil, through Microsoft today, and to the unknown victims of tomorrow—are *by design* non-objective. They help fuel the innumerable assaults on the individual's right to property and his freedom to enter into contract with others. These laws are thus an arbitrary and direct assault on the life of the productive entrepreneur.

Antitrust: A Government of Men, Not Laws

by Robert S. Getman

Forty years ago a unanimous Supreme Court declared: "The historic phrase 'a government of laws and not of men' epitomizes the distinguishing character of our political society. . . . [L]aw alone saves a society from being . . . ruled by mere brute power however disguised."

But there is an area of law in which this vital, seemingly incontrovertible principle has always been flouted: antitrust.

Imagine an Olympics where—in an attempt to "level the playing field"—no athlete was allowed to score "too many" points or to win "unreasonably." Imagine, after the event, a winner being punished for having scored "too much"—punished, at the behest of his competitors. Imagine that the very definitions of "too much" and "unreasonable" were left to the whim of each referee. Such "rules" would not "level" the field—except in the sense of leveling it to rubble, rendering all the rules arbitrary, and making athletic achievement impossible.

America's antitrust "laws" function in this same arbitrary manner. Yet they are increasingly being used against some of the most productive corporations in history, from Microsoft and Intel to McDonnell-Douglas and Northrup-Grumman. For example, the Sherman Antitrust Act—the centerpiece of the antitrust canon—prohibits businesses from engaging in "restraint of trade." But whenever anyone chooses to contract with one person rather than another, that act can be considered "restraining" trade; for that reason, the Supreme Court found it necessary to reinterpret the law as banning only "unreasonable" restraints. But this merely pushed the question back one step: What is "unreasonable"? The stark truth is that there *is* no definition; its meaning is intentionally left to the discretion of government enforcers—"the government of men."

The proscriptions of the Federal Trade Commission Act and the Clayton Act are as impossible to define as the Sherman Act's. The FTC act bans "unfair" trade practices. But what is "unfair"? Both acts seek to block monopolies. But "monopoly" itself is a legal term without precise definition. It is the rubbery notion of a company gaining "too much" of a market share. But what is "too much"? Since no producer puts a gun to buyers' heads, "too much" market share means "too many" willing buyers. (Do the federal and state attorneys-general and "consumer advocates" now attacking Microsoft, for example, wish to disintegrate or break up Windows in order to keep "too many" willing customers from getting it? And if so, does that not indicate that productive achievement and freedom are the real targets and victims of antitrust prosecutions?)

Questions such as what is "unfair" competition, an "unreasonable" trade restraint, or a "monopoly" are unanswered in antitrust—indeed they are *unanswerable.* As Alan Greenspan wrote, antitrust "is a world in which the law is so vague that businessmen have no way of knowing whether specific actions will be declared illegal until they hear the judge's verdict—after the fact."

Section III: Hatred of the Good

To define a law is to limit it; to make it deliberately undefined gives the state wide-open power to prosecute anyone, including the politically unpopular or envied—i.e., power for some men to rule others. Thus, antitrust corrupts our ideal of a "government of laws and not of men." Indeed, this power-grab starkly spotlights the ugly purpose of antitrust laws: they are designed by government officials—and jealous competitors—as guns put to the heads of "too successful" businesses.

Such laws violate our Constitution, under which *ex post facto* (retroactive) punishments are barred and undefined laws are declared "void for vagueness." These evils, inherent in antitrust laws, are magnified by the extraordinary punitiveness of those laws—which punish non-criminal violations with triple damages and criminal violations with seven-figure fines and jail time.

Our antitrust laws are truly lawless—as well as unAmerican. Indeed, they are a form of "legalized" terrorism. As philosopher Ayn Rand observed, "the threat of sudden destruction, of unpredictable retaliation for unnamed offenses . . . leaves men no other policy save one: to please the authorities . . . without standards or principles . . . . Anyone possessing such a stranglehold on businessmen possesses a stranglehold on the wealth and material resources of the country, which means: a stranglehold on the country."

Americans should recoil in horror at this vast injustice—more, Americans should rectify it, on principle, by repealing all the antitrust laws and repudiating the "deuces-wild" legal terrorism they embody.

Hatred of the Good

by Edwin A. Locke

Multi-billionaire Andrew Grant was delighted. Since the year 2000 he and his staff of engineers and computer technicians had struggled desperately to make his revolutionary hovercraft car a success. Millions of man-hours of creative effort across a span of twenty years had at last come to fruition.

The car was a technological marvel. Its air-cushion drive meant that it could travel safely over any type of terrain. It was light in weight and thus very fuel-efficient. Its patented spherical design supported by interlocking ribs composed of a new metal Grant had invented made the car exceptionally strong. This, plus a computerized laser detection system that automatically moved the car up, down, or sideways if a collision were imminent, had cut the injury rate of people using his car by 90 percent. The electronic navigation system that was tied to a positioning satellite made a driver unnecessary.

Grant's company held a 60 percent market share and it was still growing. The company had developed models for every price range and was now designing hovercraft trucks. Grant never sought publicity or acclaim but he expected that his achievement would be appreciated. He was wrong.

His "Big Three" domestic competitors who made traditional cars, Titanic, Reliable, and Strong Motor Companies, reacted with fury. They demanded an antitrust investigation, claiming that, "through a series of interlocking patents, technological innovations, and high pressure sales tactics, Grant Motors has achieved an unfair stranglehold on the automobile market." An international consortium of foreign car companies demanded a monopoly ruling by the World Court. None of these companies mentioned that the reason Grant Motors was taking away their business was that people liked its cars better than theirs.

The U.S. Automobile Dealer's Association protested that Grant Motors was "coercing" them for requiring them to order Grant's own navigation system with every car rather than installing a competing model. They failed to note that it takes two to trade, and that neither party is required to make a deal if they do not like the terms. The automobile unions screamed that Grant was causing unemployment as factory after factory owned by the Big Three was closed and union membership evaporated. They did not mention that for every Big Three factory that had closed a new, non-unionized Grant Motor factory had opened.

The Green Earth Society warned that the air turbulence caused by Grant's cars could conceivably cause global warming, global cooling, global flooding, and global drought. The predictions were backed up by computer models based on "reasonable assumptions." The society did not mention that there was no actual evidence for any of their claims.

Automotive Magazine screamed that Grant's patents were a "public trust" since his cars were in the public domain and that therefore the patents should be given away to anyone who wanted them. They did not suggest the copyrights to their magazine also be given away.

Professor Gerald Spookin, chairman of the Economics Department at Peoples University, wrote that, "Andrew Grant is another in a long line of robber barons who made their fortunes by destroying the little guy and holding the common man in the vice-like grip of their monopoly power." He did not explain how America could have become the wealthiest country in the world if its businessmen simply stole rather than created wealth.

Senator Oswald Lunt, chairman of the Joint Committee on Antitrust and Monopoly, went on TV to announce, "We will immediately begin hearings on the anticompetitive implications of the fact that Grant Motors is so successful—er, that is, dominant."

Fantasy, you say. But is it? Was our fictional Andrew Grant treated any better than John D. Rockefeller, or Andrew Carnegie, or Bill Gates? There is only one fundamental reason why great businessmen or great companies are hated, and it has nothing to do with monopoly. They are hated, as Senator Lunt above let slip, because they are good, that is, smarter, more visionary, more creative, more tenacious, more action-focused, more ambitious, and more successful than everyone else. Haters of the good do not want the less able to be raised up to the level of the great producers (which is impossible); they want the great producers to be brought down. They want to use government coercion to cripple the greatest minds—so that lesser minds will not feel inferior.

The main victims of such an evil policy, ironically,

are the less able. Thomas Edison made only a few million dollars from inventing the light bulb, but hundreds of millions of people who could not have invented it have benefited from its wonders. To limit the minds of the Thomas Edisons and Bill Gateses means to limit their capacity to create and produce wealth which means that the rest of us will be poorer as a consequence.

Attacks Against Microsoft Are Immoral

by Richard M. Salsman

On March 3 Bill Gates will testify before the United States Senate Judiciary Committee to defend Microsoft against antitrust charges. Prior to Gates's testimony, activist Ralph Nader will be mobilizing his "public citizens" to condemn Microsoft's practices. It's time for the real American public to stand up and defend—morally defend—the right of this company to its success.

Imagine a company that continually generates exceptional products. Suppose it makes such products available in ever-improved versions, at ever-lower prices. Suppose that the superiority of its products is so widely recognized that they are used in almost every industry, thereby raising productivity and living standards across the globe.

If you're a typical success-loving American, you would regard it as self-evident that this company ought to be applauded.

But now imagine that this firm is denounced as an evil "exploiter." Perhaps its out-classed competitors complain to antitrust bureaucrats, who seek to harness this company. The firm's ability to gain market share by creating the best products is condemned as "predatory." It is ordered to allow its competition to catch up. The firm is ordered to sign an oxymoronic "consent decree"— which is deliberately made vague enough so that if the firm shows new signs of racing ahead, the bureaucrats can keep prosecuting it until it is fully reined in.

Now, stop imagining. This is what has been happening to Microsoft, whose trailblazing Windows is the operating system for most personal computers today.

The latest instance of this attack on achievement is the recent court decision prohibiting Microsoft from incorporating its new Internet browser into Windows. Microsoft wants to sell that software, Explorer, as an integral element of Windows. This is a healthy economic evolution, common to all successful products. Automobiles, for example, fitted only with the basics at the turn of the century, were later enhanced with windows, upholstery, carpeting, power steering, radios, and air conditioning. The results were improved cars at lower prices. Had the manufacturers of carpeting or air conditioning been allowed to charge "unfair competition," we would still be driving bare-bones cars.

But that is exactly the charge the Justice Department now wants to enshrine in the computer field. It claims that by offering Explorer only as part of Windows, Microsoft has an "unfair advantage" over the makes of other browsers.

According to the antitrusters, Microsoft should not set the conditions of sale for its own product. It should rather be compelled to make its innovations available on whatever terms the government sets—on whatever terms benefit those who did not, and could not, match Microsoft's achievement.

Many people ask: If Microsoft's products are so demonstrably good, why is the company under assault? The answer is: precisely *because* its products are good. Does

Microsoft have a unique advantage by being able to package its browser with Windows? *Of course.* It has *earned* that advantage, because it, and no one else, developed Windows into a leading product. If its competitors want the same benefit, let them make a product equal to Windows. If buyers do not like the terms Microsoft is asking, they are completely free to patronize Microsoft's competitors. What they should *not* be free to do is to have Microsoft while eating it too.

All the prattle about "anti-competitive practices" means only one thing: Microsoft is too competent. Antitrust law is a tool to enforce the claims of any second-rater against any innovator. If you invent something so good that the market clamors for it and makes you wealthy, you are deemed a "monopolist" because your competitors are "shut out" of this market—the market *you* have created.

Microsoft is only the latest in a long line of victims of the unjust antitrust laws. From ALCOA in the 1950s to IBM in the 1970s to Wal-Mart in the 1980s, the government's goal has always been the same: prosecute an exceptional firm that is growing rich, not through theft or fraud, but through superior production and voluntary trade.

Microsoft should be cheered for taking an unusually firm stand against the Justice Department. But company officials are focusing on the wrong issue. Their basic argument should not be that the public benefits from the unfettered freedom of the best producers. This argument is true, but is not fundamental—and the antitrusters know it.

Microsoft needs to make the *moral* case for economic freedom. It needs to uphold the moral right to reap the rewards of one's achievements—the moral right to soar as high as one's talents take one—the moral right to succeed and not be shackled to others' non-success. The principle to defend is that ability should be a source of reward, not a cause of punishment—a principle upon which America was built, and a principle of which antitrust law is an obscene mockery.

This is the position that will free Microsoft—and all other producers—from the envious clutches of the success-haters.

The Brain Thieves

by Robert S. Getman

Horror movies terrify us with nightmarish plots in which aliens take over humans' brains and thus enslave their bodies. Today, Intel Corporation is a victim of just such a nightmare—with the Federal Trade Commission cast as the real-life "brain thief."

The FTC claims that because Intel is the "dominant" manufacturer of personal computer CPU's (the computer's "brain"), the company must be forced to give actual and would-be competitors a "fair" share of its patented technology and know-how. Intel is being compelled to give away what it has created—its brainchild—*because* the other companies are needy. The FTC's position is tantamount to this: the more that competitors *need* Intel's technology, the *less* Intel owns it.

What is the FTC's legal weapon in this case? It is an obscure antitrust concept, the "essential facilities" doctrine, which holds that if so-called monopolists produce something supposedly unique or "essential," it will effectively be declared public property, to which all comers must be given access. As unjust as this doctrine is (and our courts have rarely invoked it), it is particularly inappropriate as applied to patents—intellectual property established by our *Constitution*—which by their nature are *meant* to confer a "monopoly," in order to recognize an owner's exclusive right to his invention and thereby do him justice.

Section III: Hatred of the Good

Yet even the FTC doesn't claim that Intel's market "dominance" was attained by force or fraud; it simply argues that Intel is too successful at *inventing* technology that is in great demand by customers. When not referring to coercive, government-sheltered franchises, the term "monopoly" boils down to: success in a free market. For this "sin" of success, says the FTC, Intel must be made to sacrifice. It must be forced to share its creations with any have-not, on the FTC's terms. Indeed, the FTC even declares that if sued by its competitors, Intel cannot treat them less favorably than before—which means that the government is seeking to establish in law the tenet of turning the other cheek.

There are few starker examples than this lawsuit of our legal system's adoption of Marx's slogan "From each according to his ability, to each according to his need." Yet Americans would certainly oppose Thomas Edison's being hobbled for "over-invention." We would never support cutting Edison's patent rights on his lightbulb—because it is so "essential"—at the urging of gaslight-makers. Surely, it isn't part of the "American Dream" that too much success is a sin, or that a government agency is morally entitled to prosecute those it deems guilty of that sin. Such egalitarian leveling *poisons* the "pursuit of happiness," which lies at the heart of that dream.

Worse, because antitrust prevents our most successful producers from acting to maintain (let alone enhance) their "monopolies," we are forcing them to destroy their own achievements.

The evils of antitrust law are magnified enormously by its deliberate ambiguity. Most people do not realize the virtually unlimited powers government grabs as a result of the law's failure to precisely define unlawful conduct. As Alan Greenspan wrote, antitrust "is a world in which the law is so vague that businessmen have no way of knowing whether specific actions will be declared illegal until they hear the judge's verdict—after the fact."

Crucial terms like "unfair competition" and "monopolist" are kept vague *on purpose,* to accommodate the government's demand that antitrust law be "elastic." This subjectivity empowers the state to find almost any thriving business guilty of an antitrust infraction—and makes antitrust laws incompatible with the principles of a free society. (Such laws flagrantly violate our Constitution, under which *ex post facto,* or retroactive, punishments are barred and undefined laws are ruled "void for vagueness.")

The FTC's attempted brain theft imperils not just Intel, but anyone with proprietary knowledge or intellectual property. It threatens anyone who has ambition enough to enjoy "too much" success. We must awake from this legal nightmare. In the name of whatever ambition you hold dear, urge lawmakers to revoke the FTC's antitrust powers and to reject its cynical strategy to "have the producers and eat them too." Else the next brain the bureaucrats steal—if you're productive and successful—could be yours.

Making Money, Not Giving It Away, Is a Virtue

by Andrew Bernstein

There is a grave injustice being committed with respect to the praise Bill Gates is receiving for his decision to give away his $100 billion fortune during his lifetime. Gates does not deserve moral credit for giving away his wealth—but for having produced it in the first place.

According to a spokesman for the Gates foundations, the Microsoft chairman considers Andrew Carnegie his role model in philanthropy. Gates has initiated a plan to give computers to 10,000 libraries, many of which are the same ones built originally by Carnegie.

But men such as Carnegie, Gates, and others like them—John D. Rockefeller, James J. Hill, J. P. Morgan—are individuals who possess a rare virtue: the ability to create wealth on an enormous scale. They manufactured steel, produced oil, built railroads, established banks, or designed software. Business giants like these dramatically solved the problem of production—the problem that plagued mankind throughout its history, and that still plagues the impoverished, non-capitalist nations of the world.

This productivity makes human life possible. It cannot be sufficiently stressed that business production is a life-giving activity. Bill Gates's fortune represents $100 billion of additional value that *did not exist before*—value that has made people $100 billion better off than they would have been without his efforts.

Bill Gates is a genius in his field. In the amount of firsthand thinking required, his creativity equals that of such artistic geniuses as Shakespeare and Michelangelo. The software created by Microsoft enhances the lives of millions of people who use it, directly or indirectly. Just think of all the amazing efficiencies you can achieve today with a computer that would not be possible without the work of Bill Gates. Just think of how the entire "information revolution"—spurred by innovators like Gates—is advancing our standard of living.

The point is not merely that wealth must be created before it can be distributed. There is a fundamental moral issue here: the individual's right to his own life. That is, Carnegie held that wealthy individuals had a "divine duty" to give away their money while they still lived. He concluded: "The man who dies thus rich dies disgraced." But why is it a "disgrace" to die with the money that one has earned? Why is it a "disgrace" to spend it on oneself—or to leave it to one's family? Philanthropists like Carnegie believe that people have a duty to sacrifice themselves for others. But if so, what has become of the individual's "inalienable right to life, liberty and the pursuit of happiness"?

The political right of an individual to his own life is an essential principle of liberty. And it rests on the *moral* rightness of acting to sustain one's own life, which includes generating the material wealth life requires. The only disgrace for a healthy individual is to live a parasitic, non-productive life—to be a bum or a wastrel or a cheat.

To redistribute wealth from those who have produced it to those who have not requires only envy and the pointing of a gun—whether by a thief armed with a weapon or a legislator armed with a bill. It is the *creation* of wealth that demands the virtue of honest, independent effort. It is the creation of wealth that deserves tribute. And those who do it superlatively, like an Andrew Carnegie or a Bill Gates, should be regarded—by anyone who holds human life as a value—as moral heroes.

This needs to be emphatically stated in our society, where the redistributor of wealth is routinely commended, while the creator of that wealth—and the victim of the redistributors—elicits only indifference or condemnation. But producing food, automobiles, houses, medicines, etc.—not giving them away—is what human life depends on. It is the ability to produce that deserves our attention and our admiration. We must revolutionize our ethical thinking: it is the wealth-creators, not the charity-dispensers, who deserve moral praise.

Whatever benefits come from the philanthropy of a Carnegie or a Gates are marginal. Our focus should be on the primary act of generating wealth. We must learn the importance of celebrating the virtue of productivity. Our future as a productive nation requires it.

Section IV:
Fighting Racism

Racism is the lowest, most crudely primitive form of collectivism.

—Ayn Rand, "Racism,"
The Virtue of Selfishness (1964), p. 172.

Today, racism is regarded as a crime if practiced by a majority—but as an inalienable right if practiced by a minority.

—Ayn Rand, "The Age of Envy,"
Return of the Primitive (1999), p. 142.

Multiculturalism is racism in a politically correct guise. It holds that an individual's identity and personal worth are determined by ethnic/racial membership and that all cultures are of equal worth, regardless of their moral views or how they treat people. Multiculturalism holds that ethnic identity should be a central factor in educational and social policy decisions.

As the essays in this section demonstrate, multiculturalism threatens to "balkanize" this country into a collection of separatist groups competing with each other for power—triggering a tribalist war of all against all.

Apology for Slavery Will Perpetuate Racism

by Robert W. Tracinski

Consider the following scenario. You are suddenly arrested by the police one morning and charged with a crime. The crime, you are told, was committed by another man of the same color of skin—and so you will be punished for it in his place. A judge sentences you to pay a fine, perform community service, and make a public apology for the crime. Would you regard this as a gross injustice, as a form of racist persecution? In fact, a similar approach is now being promoted in the name of "racial healing."

President Clinton has indicated his support for a Congressional proposal to apologize, on behalf of the nation and the U.S. government, to "African-Americans whose ancestors suffered as slaves." This apology has been promoted as an attempt to bring "closure" to the racial divisions created by slavery. Rather than healing racism, however, this proposal would help to perpetuate it.

An apology for slavery on behalf of the nation presumes that whites today, who predominantly oppose racism, and never owned slaves, and who bear no personal responsibility for slavery, still bear a collective responsibility—a guilt they bear simply by belonging to the same race as the slaveholders of the Old South. Such an apology promotes the very idea at the root of slavery: racial collectivism.

Those who owned slaves were certainly guilty of a

grave injustice. But by what standard can other whites (many of whom are not even descendants of the slave-holders) be held responsible for their ideas and actions? By what standard can today's Americans be obliged—or even authorized—to apologize on the slaveholders' be-half? The only justification for such an approach is the idea that each member of the race can be blamed for the actions of every other member, that we are all just inter-changeable cells of the racial collective.

Critics of the proposed apology oppose it, not be-cause it embraces this racist premise, but because it does not go far enough. They want to apply the notion of ra-cial collectivism in a more "substantial" form, by increas-ing welfare and affirmative-action programs designed to compensate for the wrongs of slavery. Such compensa-tion consists of punishing random whites, by taxing them and denying them jobs and promotions, in order to re-ward random blacks. Because individual whites perse-cuted individual blacks 150 years ago, this argument goes, reparations must be paid by all whites collectively to all blacks collectively.

The ultimate result of this approach is not racial har-mony or a color-blind society, but racial warfare. Under the premise of racial collectivism, an injustice commit-ted against any member of your racial group entitles you to retaliate against any member of the perpetrator's ra-cial group. The concept of individual justice is thrown out and replaced by racial vendettas. It is precisely this kind of mentality that has devastated the Balkans, with each ethnic tribe continually exacting revenge on the other in retaliation for centuries-old grievances.

The idea of a national apology for slavery merely reinforces this same kind of racial enmity in America. By treating all whites as the stand-ins or representatives for slave-holders, it encourages the view of blacks and whites as a collective of victims pitted against an opposing and hostile collective of oppressors, with no possibility for integration or peaceful coexistence.

The only alternative to this kind of racial balkanization is to reject the notion of racial collectivism altogether and embrace the opposite principle: individualism. People should be judged based on their choices, ideas, and actions as individuals, not as "representatives" of a racial group. They should be rewarded based on their own merits—and they must not be forced to pay, or to apologize, for crimes committed by others, merely because those others have the same skin color.

Americans, both black and white, should reject the notion of a collective guilt for slavery. They should uphold the ideal of a color-blind society, based on individualism, as the real answer to racism.

Why Clinton's Race Panel Recommendations Cannot Work

by Edwin A. Locke

The long-awaited Presidential Report on race relations is out. The report reaffirmed the Clinton administration's support of affirmative action and racial and ethnic diversity. The report also argued that there should be a permanent presidential panel to promote racial harmony. The problem is, however, that racial harmony is incompatible with affirmative action and its policy of racial quotas.

Although it is now taken as a virtual axiom that the way to cure racism is through the promulgation of racial and ethnic diversity within corporations, universities, government agencies, and other institutions, the unshakable fact is that *you cannot cure racism with racism.* To accept the diversity premise underlying affirmative action means to ignore individual character or merit.

Consider the issue in the realm of work as a case in point. Taking jobs away from one group in order to compensate a second group to correct injustices caused by a third group who mistreated a fourth group at an earlier point in history (e.g., 1860) is absurd on the face of it and does not promote justice; rather, it does the opposite. Singling out one group for special favors (through affirmative action) breeds justified resentment and fuels the prejudices of racists. People are individuals; they are not interchangeable ciphers in an amorphous collective.

Consider a more concrete, though fictional, example.

Suppose that since its creation in 1936, the XYZ Corporation refused to hire redheaded men due to a quirky bias on the part of its founder. The founder now dies, and an enlightened board of directors decides that something "positive" needs to be done to compensate for past injustices and announces that, henceforth, redheads will be hired on a preferential basis. Observe that: (1) this does not help the real victims—the previously excluded redheads; (2) the newly favored redheads have not been victims of discrimination in hiring, yet unfairly benefit from it; and (3) the non-redheads who are now excluded from jobs due to the redhead preference did not cause the previous discrimination and are now unfairly made victims of it. The proper solution, of course, is simply to stop discriminating based on irrelevant factors. Although redheaded bias is not a social problem, the principle remains the same when you replace hair color with skin color.

The traditional solution to the problem of racism has been termed color-blindness. This principle is correct, but comes at the issue negatively. A better formulation of it is *individuality awareness*. In the job sphere there are only three essential things an employer needs to know about an individual applicant: (1) Does the person have the relevant ability and knowledge (or the capacity to learn readily)? (2) Is the person willing to exert the needed effort? and (3) Does the person have good character, e.g., honesty, integrity?

Some may argue that the above view is too "idealistic," in that people often make judgments of other people based on non-essential attributes such as skin color, gender, religion, nationality, etc. This, of course, does happen. But the solution is not to abandon the ideal but to implement it consistently. Thus, training and education should focus not on diversity-worship but on how to objectively assess or measure ability, motivation, and character in other people.

The proper alternative to diversity, that is, to focusing on the collective, is to focus on the individual and to treat each individual according to his or her own merits. This principle should apply in every sphere of life from business, to education, to law enforcement, to politics. Americans have always abhorred the concept of royalty, that is, granting status and privilege (and, on the other side of the same coin, inferiority and debasement) based on one's hereditary caste, because it contradicts the principle that what counts are the self-made characteristics possessed by each individual. Americans should abhor racism, *in any form*, for the same reason.

Our leaders have not had the courage to identify the proper antidote to racism and the proper alternative to racial thinking: individualism. Their belief—that you can cure racism with racial quotas—is a hopeless quest with nothing but increased conflict and injustice as the end. Here is what every parent, every teacher, and every leader should promulgate as the prime axiom of racial harmony: you are a sovereign individual human being.

The Assault on Ability

by Robert W. Tracinski

As Jesse Jackson makes news by jumping into that seething cauldron of ethnic hatreds—the Balkans—too little attention is being paid to his own campaign for creating racial conflict at home. He has been urging America to enter what he calls the "next frontier of the civil rights movement." He wants us to recognize a "right to capital."

Jackson has targeted Wall Street and Silicon Valley, claiming that investors aren't lending "enough" money to black-owned businesses, that companies are not putting "enough" blacks on their boards of directors, and that technology firms aren't hiring "enough" black engineers and computer programmers.

"Enough"—by what standard? Both Wall Street and Silicon Valley demand the highest levels of ability. To write millions of lines of software code, or to design the next generation of computer chips, or to direct a billion-dollar corporation—these are jobs requiring an unusual amount of education, experience, judgment, and intelligence. Yet these are not the criteria by which Jackson believes such individuals should be hired. He demands, instead, that they be selected by a method about as sophisticated as drawing names at random from a phone book.

Take his Silicon Valley crusade. Jackson points to the fact that blacks make up only 4 percent of the employees in the region's high-technology firms, while they constitute 8 percent of the area's population. But software companies do not pull their employees off the street at whim. They hire from a pool of educated, technically knowledgeable people. Yet according to the Department of Education, blacks make up only 5.3 percent of those who receive college degrees in engineering and computer science.

Given these statistics, it would be more rational to attribute low numbers of black computer programmers to the abysmal failure of our public schools, which have failed to prepare inner-city children for college. There may even be more innocuous explanations: Cypress Semiconductor CEO T. J. Rogers points to statistics showing that far more blacks pursue advanced degrees in medicine and education than in engineering, and asks: "If top African-American students choose to be doctors or educators instead of engineers, why blame Silicon Valley?"

But Jackson regards such considerations as irrelevant. He does not bother to ask how many blacks have the qualifications or interest to acquire these jobs. Instead, he insists that they be granted jobs in proportion to their numbers in the general population—and condemns anything less as a violation of "civil rights."

His approach to Wall Street is similar. Is he seriously suggesting that investment bankers are not greedy enough to want to make lots of money from the talents of black economic geniuses? And if there indeed are, as Jackson implies, black Warren Buffets and Bill Gateses who are being denied capital for no reason other than their skin color—why doesn't *he* organize an investment fund to profit from this enormous financial opportunity?

The answer is that Jackson does not care about business acumen or any other objective form of merit. It is precisely such qualities that he wants to override in favor of the meaningless fact of race. Jackson's demands constitute, not a fight for civil rights, but an assault on human ability.

Notice that Jackson offers no proof of racial discrimination in these fields. There are no stories of talented black programmers or financiers being turned away from potential employers. All that Jackson cites is these companies' failure to meet an arbitrarily devised racial quota. This is a particularly insidious form of the injustice inherent in "affirmative action"—under which hiring and promotion are based, not on an individual's competence, but on racial quotas. It is bad enough to put race above merit when it comes to employing people to pull levers on assembly lines. But can one imagine hiring on the basis of quotas when the job is to direct a billion-dollar conglomerate?

In the computer industry, Bill Gates looks for "supersmart" programmers, and has even purchased small software companies just to acquire their talented employees. On Wall Street, the genius of one CEO can make the difference between bankruptcy and billions. These are arenas in which human ability is paramount—precisely the reason that profit-seeking computer executives or Wall Street investors cannot afford to indulge in racial prejudice, including the kind of "reverse racism" endorsed by Jackson. They cannot afford to make business decisions based on any standard other than individual ability. If Jackson learns anything from his Serbia trip, it should be the utter irrationality of judging people by ethnic heritage.

Section V:
The Government Versus Progress

The only proper purpose of a government is to pro-tect man's rights, which means: to protect him from physical violence. A proper government is only a policeman, acting as an agent of man's self-defense, and, as such, may resort to force only against those who start the use of force. The only proper func-tions of a government are: the police, to protect you from criminals; the army, to protect you from foreign invaders; and the courts, to protect your property and contracts from breach or fraud by others.

—Ayn Rand, "Galt's Speech,"
For the New Intellectual (1961) p. 183.

The essays in this section cover a number of seemingly unrelated themes: human cloning, foreign trade, volunteerism, and rent control. In each case, however, the issue is: *the government against the individual*. Should medical science be allowed to develop human cloning technology? Do you have a duty to serve others? Should you have the right to establish the terms of use of your own property? Issues like these abound in our everyday lives. How can they be resolved?

The very fact that debates emerge over what the government should permit in regard to such issues as cloning, trade, and rent control is evidence that something is seriously amiss in our culture.

The answer in each case is to be found by reference to the principle of individual rights. These essays demonstrate how a proper government—one that respects the rights of the individual—would address, or more appropriately *not* address, these so-called crises.

Human Cloning—Yes!

by Harry Binswanger

By rejecting heavy restrictions on animal cloning, the Senate has upheld the right of free scientific inquiry. But will it cave in to the broad chorus of public figures, including the President, who demand a ban on cloning human beings?

Human cloning—everyone seems to tremble at the prospect. Why?

After all, we are not talking about a weapon of mass destruction, just the ability to produce a baby who exactly resembles, physically, someone else—a godsend for infertile couples. Where's the threat?

The fear is only partly explained by misconceptions resulting from Hollywood's treatment of cloning. In films like *Multiplicity,* cloning is presented as a sort of super-photocopying: you stand in one chamber, lights flash, and in another chamber your exact double appears. But an actual clone is not an adult but an egg cell implanted in a woman to begin a normal pregnancy.

If you were cloned today, nine months from now a woman would give birth to a baby with your genetic endowment. The cloned baby would be your identical twin, delayed a generation.

Twins of the same age do not frighten us, so why should twins separated by a generation?

Some fear the specter of mass cloning of one individual, especially cloning of sadistic monsters, as in *The*

Boys from Brazil, Ira Levin's nightmarish projection of cadres of young Hitlers spawned from the dictator's genes.

The error here is philosophical: the equation of a person with his body. A person's essential self is his mind—that in him which thinks, values, and chooses. It is one's mind, not one's genes, that governs who one is.

Man is a rational animal. As such, his identity is self-made. Man's basic choice is to think or not to think, in Ayn Rand's famous phrase, and one's conclusions, values, character will differ according to the extent and quality of his thinking.

Genes provide the capacity to reason, but the exercise and guidance of that capacity is up to each individual, from the birth of his reasoning mind in infancy through the rest of his life.

Neither genes nor physical environment nor the practices of his parents can implant ideas in a child's mind and make him accept them. Only his own self-generated thinking—or his default on that responsibility—will shape his soul.

Cloning the body will not clone the mind. A mind is inescapably under the individual's own volitional control. *The Boys from Brazil*? It was not Hitler's genes but his choices that made him a monster.

Yes, the technology of cloning can be misused. Any technology can be. In particular, parents might treat a cloned child as a reincarnation of the person he resembles rather than as a unique, separate individual. But the same wrong has always been possible in the form of parents who attempt to relive their own lives through their children.

Given the virtual panic over human cloning, and the fact that the anti-cloning contingent opposes human cloning across the board, in any quantity for any reason, the anti-cloning hysteria is clearly not generated by worry about such misuses of the technology.

The actual opposition to human cloning stems from the primordial fear of the unknown, the fear reflected in the catch-phrase: "We can't play God." But why can't we? We can and we must.

A surgeon "plays God" whenever he removes a cancer or an infected appendix rather than letting the patient die. We "play God" anytime we use our rational faculty to improve the "natural" course of events. Man's very survival is achieved by "playing God": altering the environment to produce the food, shelter, cars, and power stations that fulfill his survival needs. Not to "play God" in this context means to abandon the struggle for human life and submit uncomplainingly to whatever happens.

Human cloning would emancipate not only infertile couples but also those fearing birth defects inherited from one partner. It would extend prospective parents' control of the reproductive process—which is precisely why it is feared by the familiar phalanx of Luddites, religionists, and the merely confused.

We cannot predict what kind of life-enhancing biomedical applications, including stopping or reversing the aging process, may spin off from developing the technology of human cloning.

As humanity stands at the threshold of a wide range of exciting biomedical advances, we must not let irrational fears of the new impede the development of any

nal fears of the new impede the development of any technology that is both a value in itself and a link to the wider struggle to enhance and extend human life.

CEOs Scrubbing Graffiti? The Inverted Values of Colin Powell's "Volunteerism" Campaign

by Robert W. Tracinski

President Clinton's "volunteerism" drive was launched in the spring of 1997 in order to impose a "national sense of obligation" upon people and "to make citizen service a part of every American's life." This campaign is now focusing on businesses, aiming—in General Colin Powell's words—to "give them a guilt trip." For what? For devoting their efforts to productive achievement.

In a terrible moral inversion, businesses are being condemned for creating the products upon which our lives depend—and are being extolled for abandoning such activities in favor of scrubbing graffiti off inner-city sidewalks.

Consider the case of a typical corporate target, the pharmaceutical firm Glaxo Wellcome. This company manufactures medicines that treat such illnesses as congestive heart failure, epileptic seizures, Parkinson's disease, and lung cancer. Any rational person would assume that it is the production of such valuable drugs that ought to generate pride on the part of the company and praise on the part of the public.

The service-promoters, however, assume otherwise. They want the company to seek penance for its profit-making activities. They don't want it to devote such single-minded effort to researching and marketing new drugs. Instead, they want Glaxo Wellcome to give workers time off for "community service." They want the employees to leave their laboratories and boardrooms and go out into the streets and the parks. They want them to man soup kitchens, pick up litter, and carry bedpans—to engage in any activity, that is, whose defining characteristic is the absence of self-interest.

When these "volunteerists" concentrated on the schools, they repudiated the idea that each student ought to pursue an education in order to better himself by acquiring the knowledge necessary for his future life. Instead, these students were to be taught to surrender their personal goals and embrace selfless service. "Every young American should learn the joy and the duty of serving," Clinton said.

Now that the target is business, the essential demands are the same. The individual must accommodate the interests of others and sacrifice his own.

Compounding the injustice of the demands for servitude is the corporate world's craven capitulation. Many companies are appeasing the volunteerists by apologizing for devoting so much time on profit-making work. Glaxo Wellcome, for example, has pledged to pay its employees for 300,000 hours spent as "community servants." Prudential has sent its workers on missions to beautify highways and to collect linens for day camp. Other companies have made similar concessions.

Not only are such programs growing, but the "volunteerists" have the perverse audacity to promote "citizen service" as part of "Americanism." America was founded on the principle of individualism—the principle that the individual has a political and moral right to pursue his own happiness, rather than be indentured to the needs of society. Those complying with the government's exhortation to sacrifice their work for the sake of the community—whether they do it "voluntarily" or not—are servants. They are toiling for the benefit of others, with no reward, no payment, no self-interested purpose—only the purpose of placating those with an inverted morality that regards self-interested production as evil and selfless servitude as good.

This creed holds that to produce wealth deserves no moral credit—but to redistribute it, does. Three hundred thousand manhours spent on developing new drugs, in this view, have no moral value—but those same hours devoted to cleaning the streets, do. Anything done to advance your own life is morally suspect—but anything done to serve others is noble.

This belief is a complete reversal of the truth. All productive work—from that of a Fortune 500 CEO to that of a janitor—is selfish. The people who perform such work are engaged in the primary business of life: the business of producing wealth—from life-saving drugs to computer operating systems. They are the ones who make human life and progress possible.

Thanks to the twisted views of the volunteerism advocates, however, these people find themselves the objects of a campaign of guilt. The productive giants who create new businesses and previously unimagined wealth are told that they must "give back to the community"— as if their creations constitute theft, for which they must be punished by being sentenced to "community service."

This campaign against the wealth-producers will not

cease until society stops regarding profit as a sin and production as a vice—and until business stops trying to atone to the world for its virtues.

Why Rent Control Is Immoral

by Michael S. Berliner

Rent controls don't work, and everybody knows it. Rent controls create shortages and decrease the quality of housing. Yet the activists for rent control don't care that it doesn't work. They—and much of the public—think that rent controls are "humanitarian." After all, isn't the government helping out poor people and keeping them out of the clutches of greedy, gouging landlords? What drives these activists are not issues of practicality but issues of *morality*. They are possessed by the same moral fervor that still leads leftists to claim that socialism is the best system, despite the collapse of the USSR and all the model socialist economies.

In fact, there is nothing moral about rent controls.

Rent controls violate your rights. They are a gun at your head. As an apartment owner, you have the moral right to decide the price at which you'll offer a unit for rent. The government has no right to dictate to you what rate you can offer. Of course, it is legally *empowered* to do this; it is legally empowered to do whatever it can enact into law and get upheld by the courts. But that doesn't make it moral. Slavery was legal at one time, but it was never moral. And rent controls are nothing less than enslavement of the property owner.

In a free society, no government (local, state, or federal) has the right to interfere with the choices of people to do business with each other. It should no more tell a landlord what price to offer than it should tell a prospective tenant how much he can spend on rent. Both the landlord and the tenant have the moral right to "just say no" to the other's offer. That's freedom.

Government is an institution of physical force: police, courts, army. Government has a *monopoly* on the use of such force: it's the only institution legally empowered to enforce its decisions by the threat of taking your money or putting you behind bars. Rent control is the government putting a gun at the head of people trying to make voluntary contracts with each other. That's why rent controls violate the rights of *everyone*, not just landlords. It's never "humane" to prevent people from acting on their own judgment. It's never "humane" to turn people into slaves to someone else's desires.

But from their supposedly high moral plane, the advocates of rent control make a lot of serious charges which do require answers:

1. "Only the landlord has a choice, because he controls the apartment that the tenant needs and thus he has the tenant over a barrel."

ANSWER: The *tenant* controls the rent that the landlord needs; that's always what's involved in a contract: each party has a value the other wants, and they trade their values to mutual advantage. Neither party has a *right* to the other's values: landlords have no divine right to a customer or to certain levels of rent (they're free to lower their offers or invest their money elsewhere), and tenants have no right to demand housing (they're free to seek alternative housing). Of course, the advocates of rent control recognize the importance of housing (and medicine and food) and thus feel morally justified in forcing people to provide those things to the "needy." But their position is the exact opposite of the moral position. The more valuable and important the product, the more you should be rewarded—not punished—for supplying it! Need is not a claim.

2. "Human rights are more important than property rights."

ANSWER: Property rights are human rights, and very basic ones. They are the rights of human beings to use their own property. As Ayn Rand wrote in *Capitalism: The Unknown Ideal:* "Without property rights, no other rights are possible. Since man has to sustain his life by his own effort, the man who has no right to the product of his effort has no means to sustain his life. The man who produces while others dispose of his product, is a slave."

3. "Rent controls are perfectly legitimate because this is a democracy, and rent controls have been voted in."

ANSWER: It makes no difference how popular a law is; it can still be a violation of your rights. Just because the majority votes away your property, that doesn't give it a moral right to do so. If a neighbor sneaks into your house and takes some money out of your wallet to help pay his rent, that's theft; well, there's no moral difference if a *group* of your neighbors get together and vote away your money to help pay their rents; that's merely "legalized theft." If majority rule were the only basis for deciding what the government can do, then 51 percent of the people could legitimately vote to enslave or even kill the other 49 percent. Hitler was voted into office and had great popular support. All tyrannies are wrong, including tyranny by the majority. The voters don't own your life or your property.

4. "Landlords are just being selfish by wanting higher rents."

ANSWER: Why is it okay for tenants to be selfish by wanting *lower* rents? In fact, there's nothing wrong with being selfish—*rationally selfish*. Selfishness means that you live for your own happiness, not that of others. You want the highest rent you can get, and tenants want the best apartment for the least possible rent. Neither party should be altruistic: the landlord shouldn't say "you can have this apartment for less than you're willing to spend," nor should the tenant say "I'll pay you more than you're willing to take, just to make you happy." Being selfish means you don't sacrifice yourself to others or sacrifice others to yourself. It means that you—and everyone—live independently, trading value for value.

Property owners should not be apologetic for what they do; they should be proud. They should stand up for their right to control their own property. They should reject the claim—inherited from Marxism—that they are "evil exploiters." They should not try to appease their opponents by compromising. It doesn't work; in fact, appeasement of one's enemies just encourages them. "In any collaboration between two men (or two groups) who hold different basic principles," wrote Ayn Rand, "it is the more evil or irrational one who wins." It isn't possible to compromise with people who want to dictate your life. By agreeing to *any* of their demands, you concede their right to your property and give them a complete victory.

Even the Russians seem to be discovering that an economy run by dictatorial decrees (a "command" economy) destroys freedom. Isn't it about time that our own politicians and tenants learn the same lesson?

Section VI:
Celebrating Production

The best aspect of Christmas is the aspect usually decried by the mystics: the fact that Christmas has become commercialized. *The gift-buying . . . stimulates an enormous outpouring of ingenuity in the creation of products devoted to a single purpose: to give men pleasure. And the street decorations put up by department stores and other institutions—the Christmas trees, the winking lights, the glittering colors—provide the city with a spectacular display, which only "commercial greed" could afford to give us.*

—Ayn Rand, The Objectivist Calendar,
December 1976.

In the health care system, in antitrust laws, in environmental regulations, in "affirmative action" statutes, and in myriad other ways, the state attacks the rights of individuals to think, create, produce, and prosper.

But while the forces of collectivism and "big government" seem to pose increasingly formidable obstacles for the creator and the producer, creation and production do occur nevertheless—relying in large measure upon heroic individuals working within the vestigial freedom that remains in America. These accomplishments are attained in the face of increasingly irrational, unjust, and onerous barriers (as preceding essays have illustrated)—

and are far less than could be achieved in a full, free, capitalist society. But rational, productive achievement in any context should serve as a source of pride. In the context of modern welfare-state America, these achievements are even more a cause for celebration—given the obstacles that capitalists must overcome in order to produce and prosper.

These concluding essays focus on celebrating the achievements of those whom Ayn Rand called "the men of the mind."

Time to Celebrate Man's Mind

by Fredric Hamber

It is fitting that the most productive nation on earth should have a holiday to honor its work. The high standard of living that Americans enjoy is hard earned and well deserved. But the term "Labor Day" is a misnomer. What we should celebrate is not sweat and toil, but the power of man's mind to reason, invent, and create.

Several centuries ago, providing the basic necessities for one's survival was a matter of daily drudgery for most people. But Americans today enjoy conveniences undreamed of by medieval kings. Every day brings some new useful household gadget, or a new software system to increase our productivity, or a breakthrough in biotechnology.

So, it is worth asking: Why do Americans have no unique holiday to celebrate the creators, inventors, and entrepreneurs who have made all of this wealth possible—the men of the mind?

The answer lies in the dominant intellectual view of the nature of work. Most of today's intellectuals, influenced by several generations of Marxist political philosophy, still believe that wealth is created by sheer physical toil. But the high standard of living we enjoy today is not due to our musculature and physical stamina. Many animals have been much stronger. We owe our relative affluence not to muscle power, but to brain power.

Brain power is given a left-handed acknowledgement

in today's fashionable aphorism that we are living in an "information age" in which education and knowledge are the keys to economic success. The implication of this idea, however, is that prior to the invention of the silicon chip, humans were able to flourish as brainless automatons.

The importance of knowledge to progress is not some recent trend, but a metaphysical fact of human nature. Man's mind is his tool of survival and the source of every advance in material well-being throughout history, from the harnessing of fire, to the invention of the plough, to the discovery of electricity, to the invention of the latest anti-cancer drug.

Contrary to the Marxist premise that wealth is created by laborers and "exploited" by those at the top of the pyramid of ability, it is those at the top, the best and the brightest, who increase the value of the labor of those at the bottom. Under capitalism, even a man who has nothing to trade but physical labor gains a huge advantage by leveraging the fruits of minds more creative than his. The labor of a construction worker, for example, is made more productive and valuable by the inventors of the jackhammer and the steam shovel, and by the far-sighted entrepreneurs who market and sell such tools to his employer. The work of an office clerk, as another example, is made more efficient by the men who invented copiers and fax machines. By applying human ingenuity to serve men's needs, the result is that physical labor is made less laborious and more productive.

An apt symbol of the theory that sweat and muscle are the creators of economic value can be seen in those

Soviet-era propaganda posters depicting man as a mind-less muscular robot with an expressionless, cookie-cutter face. In practice, that theory led to chronic famines in a society unable to produce even the most basic necessities.

A culture thrives to the extent that it is governed by reason and science and stagnates to the extent that it is governed by brute force. But the importance of the mind in human progress has been evaded by most of this century's intellectuals. Observe, for example, George Orwell's novel *1984*, which depicts a totalitarian state that still, somehow, is a fully advanced technological society. Orwell projects the impossible: technology without the minds to produce it.

The best and brightest minds are always the first to either flee a dictatorship in a "brain drain" or to cease their creative efforts. A totalitarian regime can force some men to perform muscular labor; it cannot force a genius to create, nor force a businessman to make rational decisions. A slave owner can force a man to pick peanuts; only under freedom would a George Washington Carver discover ways to increase crop yields.

What Americans should celebrate is the spark of genius in the scientist who first identifies a law of physics, in the inventor who uses that knowledge to create a new engine or telephonic device, and in the businessmen who daily translate their ideas into tangible wealth.

On Labor Day, let us honor the true root of production and wealth: the human mind.

July 4 Celebrates America's and the West's Core Values

by Edwin A. Locke

Why should we celebrate the Fourth of July? Because America—as the greatest product of Western civilization—is the greatest country in the world. But it cannot remain great unless we understand the causes of its greatness.

In this age of diversity-worship, it is considered axiomatic that all cultures and countries are equal. Western culture, it is declared, is in no way superior to that of any other, not even to tribes of cannibals. To deny the equality of all cultures, claim the intellectuals, is to be guilty of the most heinous of intellectual sins: "ethnocentrism." It is to flout the "sacred" (and false) principle of cultural relativism. I disagree with the relativists—absolutely.

There are three fundamental respects in which Western culture is objectively the best. The core values and achievements of Western civilization—the values that made America great—are:

1. *Reason.* The Greeks were the first to identify philosophically that knowledge is gained through reason and logic as opposed to mysticism (faith, tradition, revelation, dogma). It would take two millennia, including a Dark Ages and a Renaissance, before the full implications of Greek thought would be realized. The rule of reason reached its zenith in the West in the 18th century—the Age of Enlightenment. "For the first time in modern history," writes one philosopher, "an authentic

respect for reason became the mark of an entire culture." America is the epitome of Enlightenment thought.

2. *Individual Rights.* An indispensable achievement leading to the Enlightenment was the recognition of the concept of individual rights. John Locke demonstrated that individuals do not exist to serve governments, but rather that governments exist to protect individuals. The individual, said Locke, has an inalienable right to life, liberty, and the pursuit of his own happiness. This was the founding philosophy of America. (America made a disastrous error by tolerating slavery, which originated elsewhere, but it was too incongruent with America's core principles of reason and rights to endure and was corrected in the name of those principles.)

3. *Science and Technology.* The triumph of reason and rights made possible the full development and application of science and technology and ultimately modern industrial society. Once man's mind was freed from the tyranny of religious dogma, and man's productive capacity was freed from the tyranny of state control, scientific and technological progress followed in several interdependent steps. Men began to understand the laws of nature. They invented machinery. They engaged in large-scale production, that is, the creation of wealth. This wealth, in turn, financed and motivated further invention and production. As a result, horse-and-buggies were replaced by automobiles, wagon tracks by steel rails, and candles by electricity. The dictator and the Grand Inquisitor were replaced by Thomas Edison and John D. Rockerfeller. At last, after millennia of struggle, man became the master of his environment.

The result of these core achievements was an increase in freedom, wealth, health, comfort, and life expectancy unprecedented in the history of the world. These Western achievements were greatest in the country where the principles of reason and rights were implemented most consistently—the United States of America. In contrast, it was precisely in those (third world) countries which did not embrace reason, rights, and technology where people suffered (and still suffer) most from both natural and man-made disasters (famine, poverty, illness, dictatorship) and where life-expectancy was (and is) lowest. It is said that primitives live "in harmony with nature," but in reality they are simply victims of the vicissitudes of nature—if some dictator does not kill them first.

The greatness of America is not an "ethnocentric" prejudice; it is an objective fact. This assessment is based on the only proper standard for judging a culture or a society: the degree to which its core values are pro- or anti-life. Pro-life cultures acknowledge and respect man's nature as a rational being who must discover and create the conditions which his survival and happiness require—which means that they advocate reason, rights (freedom), and technological progress.

Despite its undeniable triumphs, America is by no means secure. Its core principles are under attack from every direction—by religious zealots who want to undermine the separation of church and state and by its own intellectuals, who are denouncing reason in the name of skepticism, rights in the name of special entitlements, and progress in the name of environmentalism. We are heading rapidly toward the destruction of our core values and the dead end of nihilism. The core values and achievements of the West and of America must be asserted proudly and defended to the death. Our lives depend on them.

Thanksgiving: The Producer's Holiday

by Gary Hull

Thanksgiving celebrates man's ability to produce. The cornucopia filled with exotic flowers and delicious fruits, the savory turkey with aromatic trimmings, the mouth-watering pies, the colorful decorations—it's all a testament to the creation of wealth.

Thanksgiving is a uniquely American holiday, because this country was the first to create and to value material abundance. It is America that has been the beacon for anyone wanting to escape from poverty and misery. It is America that generated the unprecedented flood of goods that washed away centuries of privation. It is America, by establishing the precondition of production —political freedom—that was able to unleash the dynamic, productive energy of its citizens.

This should be a source of pride to every self-supporting individual. It is what Thanksgiving is designed to commemorate. But there are those, motivated by hatred for human comfort and happiness, who want to make Thanksgiving into a day of national guilt. We should be ashamed, they say, for consuming a disproportionate share of the world's food supply. Our affluence, they say, constitutes a depletion of the "planet's resources." The building of dams, the use of fossil fuels, the driving of sports utility vehicles—they insist—are cause, not for celebration, but for atonement. What if, they all wail, the rest of the world consumed the way

Americans do?

If only that were to happen—we would have an Atlantis. For it would mean that the production of wealth would have multiplied. Man can consume only what he first produces. All production is an act of creation. It is the creation of wealth where nothing before existed—nothing useful to man. America transformed a once-desolate wilderness into farms, supermarkets, and air-conditioned houses, not by taking those goods away from some have-nots, nor by "consuming" the "world's resources"—but by reshaping valueless elements of nature into a form beneficial to human beings.

Since human survival is not automatic, man's life depends on successful production. From food and clothing to science and art, every act of production requires thought. And the greater the creation, the greater is the required thinking.

This virtue of productiveness is what Thanksgiving is supposed to recognize. Sadly, this is a virtue rejected not only by the attackers of this holiday, but by its alleged defenders as well.

Many Americans make Thanksgiving into a religious festival. They agree with Lincoln, who, upon declaring Thanksgiving a national holiday in 1863, said that "we have been the recipients of the choicest bounties of heaven." They ascribe our material abundance to God's efforts, not man's.

That view is a slap in the face of any person who has worked an honest day in his life. The appropriate values for this holiday are not faith and charity, but thought and production. The proper thanks for one's wealth goes not to some mystical deity but to *oneself,* if one has earned that wealth.

The liberal tells us that the food on our Thanksgiving plate is the result of mindless, meaningless labor. The conservative tells us that it is the result of supernatural grace. Neither believes that it represents an individual's achievement.

But wealth is not generated by sheer muscle; India, for example, has far more manual laborers than does the United States. Nor is it generated by praying for God's blessing; Iran, for example, is far more religious. If the liberal and conservative views of wealth are correct, why aren't those countries awash in riches?

Wealth is the result of individual thought and effort. And each individual is morally entitled to keep, and enjoy, the consequences of such thought and effort. He should not feel guilty for his own success, or for the failures of others.

There is a spiritual need fed by the elaborate meal, fine china and crystal, and the presence of cherished guests. It is the self-esteem that a productive person feels at the realization that his thinking and energy have made consumption possible.

Come Thanksgiving Day, when some success-hating commentator condemns America for being the world's leading consumer, tell him that he is evading the underlying fact: that this country is the world's leading *producer.* And then, as you sit down to dinner, celebrate the spiritual significance of the holiday by raising a toast to the virtue of your own productive ability and to America's productive giants, past and present.

Why Christmas Should Be More Commercial

by Leonard Peikoff

Christmas in America is an exuberant display of human ingenuity, capitalist productivity, and the enjoyment of life. Yet all of these are castigated as "materialistic"; the real meaning of the holiday, we are told, is assorted Nativity tales and altruist injunctions (e.g., love thy neighbor) that no one takes seriously.

In fact, Christmas as we celebrate it today is a 19th-century American invention. The freedom and prosperity of post–Civil War America created the happiest nation in history. The result was the desire to celebrate, to revel in the goods and pleasures of life on earth. Christmas (which was not a federal holiday until 1870) became the leading American outlet for this feeling.

Historically, people have always celebrated the winter solstice as the time when the days begin to lengthen, indicating the earth's return to life. Ancient Romans feasted and reveled during the festival of Saturnalia. Early Christians condemned these Roman celebrations—they were waiting for the end of the world and had only scorn for earthly pleasures. By the fourth century, the pagans were worshipping the god of the sun on December 25, and the Christians came to a decision: if you can't stop 'em, join 'em. They claimed (contrary to known fact) that the date was Jesus' birthday, and usurped the solstice holiday for their Church.

Even after the Christians stole Christmas, they were

ambivalent about it. The holiday was inherently a pro-life festival of earthly renewal, but the Christians preached renunciation, sacrifice, and concern for the next world, not this one. As Cotton Mather, an 18th-century clergyman, put it: "Can you in your consciences think that our Holy Savior is honored by mirth? . . . Shall it be said that at the birth of our Savior . . . we take time . . . to do actions that have much more of hell than of heaven in them?"

Then came the major developments of 19th-century capitalism: industrialization, urbanization, the triumph of science—all of it leading to easy transportation, efficient mail delivery, the widespread publishing of books and magazines, new inventions making life comfortable and exciting, and the rise of entrepreneurs who understood that the way to make a profit was to produce something good and sell it to a mass market.

For the first time, the giving of gifts became a major feature of Christmas. Early Christians denounced gift-giving as a Roman practice, and Puritans called it diabolical. But Americans were not to be deterred. Thanks to capitalism, there was enough wealth to make gifts possible, a great productive apparatus to advertise them and make them available cheaply, and a country so content that men wanted to reach out to their friends and express their enjoyment of life. The whole country took with glee to giving gifts on an unprecedented scale.

Santa Claus is a thoroughly American invention. There was a St. Nicholas long ago and a feeble holiday connected with him (on December 5). In 1822, an American named Clement Clarke Moore wrote a poem about a visit from St. Nick. It was Moore (and a few other New Yorkers) who invented St. Nick's physical appearance and personality, came up with the idea that Santa travels on Christmas Eve in a sleigh pulled by reindeer, comes down the chimney, stuffs toys in the kids' stockings, then goes back to the North Pole.

Of course, the Puritans denounced Santa as the Anti-Christ, because he pushed Jesus to the background. Furthermore, Santa implicitly rejected the whole Christian ethics. He did not denounce the rich and demand that they give everything to the poor; on the contrary, he gave gifts to rich and poor children alike. Nor is Santa a champion of Christian mercy or unconditional love. On the contrary, he is for justice—Santa gives only to good children, not to bad ones.

All the best customs of Christmas, from carols to trees to spectacular decorations, have their root in pagan ideas and practices. These customs were greatly amplified by American culture, as the product of reason, science, business, worldliness, and egoism, i.e., the pursuit of happiness.

America's tragedy is that its intellectual leaders have typically tried to replace happiness with guilt by insisting that the spiritual meaning of Christmas is religion and self-sacrifice for Tiny Tim or his equivalent. But the spiritual must start with recognizing reality. Life requires reason, selfishness, capitalism; that is what Christmas should celebrate—and really, underneath all the pretense, that is what it does celebrate. It is time to take the Christ out of Christmas and turn the holiday into a guiltlessly egoistic, pro-reason, this-worldly, commercial celebration.

Author Biographies

Michael S. Berliner, Ph.D.

Dr. Berliner is the senior advisor to the Ayn Rand Archive. He was the executive director of the Ayn Rand Institute from its founding in 1985 to January 2000. Dr. Berliner is the editor of *Letters of Ayn Rand* (Penguin Dutton, 1995) and *Russian Writings on Hollywood by Ayn Rand* (ARI Press, 1999), and is author of Penguin's "Teacher's Guide to *Anthem*." His editorials on such topics as Western civilization and multiculturalism have been published in the *Los Angeles Times* and other major newspapers. He holds a Ph.D. in philosophy and taught philosophy and philosophy of education for many years at California State University, Northridge, where he served as chairman of the Department of Social and Philosophical Foundations of Education.

Andrew Bernstein, Ph.D.

Dr. Bernstein is an adjunct professor of philosophy at Pace University and at the State University of New York at Purchase. He is the author of the "Teacher's Guide to *The Fountainhead*," published by Penguin, is a member of the Speakers Bureau of the Ayn Rand Institute, and has spoken at many universities, including Harvard, Stanford, and the University of Chicago.

Harry Binswanger, Ph.D.

Dr. Binswanger is a longtime associate of Ayn Rand, and has taught philosophy at the City University of New

York, Hunter College, from 1972 to 1979. During the 1980s, he was editor of *The Objectivist Forum*, a bi-monthly journal devoted to Ayn Rand's philosophy. He is currently professor of philosophy at the Objectivist Graduate Center of the Ayn Rand Institute. He is the author of *The Biological Basis of Teleological Concepts* (ARI Press, 1990) and editor of *The Ayn Rand Lexicon* (New American Library) and of the second edition of Ayn Rand's *Introduction to Objectivist Epistemology* (New American Library). A regular speaker at universities, he has given more than 70 talks at some 40 universities on a wide variety of topics in philosophy and politics, from "The Primacy of Existence" to "'Buy American' Is Un-American."

Yaron Brook, Ph.D.

Dr. Brook is the president and executive director of the Ayn Rand Institute. As an entrepreneur, he founded three companies, including Lyceum International (a firm specializing in Objectivist conferences and distance-learning courses) and BH Equity Research, a venture capital consulting firm in San Jose, California. Dr. Brook has lectured extensively in the United States and abroad on issues related to finance, banking, regulation, corporate governance, and ethics. Dr. Brook was an assistant professor of finance at Santa Clara University in Santa Clara, California, where he received numerous teaching awards.

Robert S. Getman

Mr. Getman is a business lawyer in private practice in

New York City, and a senior writer for the Ayn Rand Institute in Marina del Rey, California.

Fredric Hamber

Mr. Hamber is a senior writer for the Ayn Rand Institute.

David Harriman

Mr. Harriman has worked as a physicist for the U.S. Department of Defense and taught philosophy at California State University, San Bernardino. He is the editor of *Journals of Ayn Rand* and a senior writer for the Ayn Rand Institute. He has lectured on the scientific revolution, the concept of "space," and the influence of Kantian philosophy on modern physics. He is currently writing a book, "The Anti-Copernican Revolution and the Fall of Physics."

Gary Hull, Ph.D.

Dr. Hull is director of the Program on Values and Ethics in the Marketplace at Duke University. He has advised major corporations and lectured to business groups throughout the country, such as The Young Presidents' Organization and the San Jose State University College of Business Alumni Association. Dr. Hull has appeared on radio and television as an expert on business ethics, and for years was a guest host for *The Leonard Peikoff Radio Show*. He has spoken on Ayn Rand's philosophy of reason and rational selfishness at numerous colleges throughout the country, including Harvard, the University of Virginia, the University of

Texas at Austin, and the University of Wisconsin.

Dr. Hull is the coeditor of *The Ayn Rand Reader* and has published articles in, among others, the *Los Angeles Times*, *Orange County Register*, *Philadelphia Inquirer*, *Chicago Tribune*, and *The Intellectual Activist*.

Edwin A. Locke, Ph.D.

Dr. Locke is a professor of business and management, and of psychology at the University of Maryland, and has had more than 200 chapters and articles published in professional journals on subjects such as leadership, job satisfaction, incentives, and the philosophy of science. He is internationally known for his work on human motivation. He is the author of such books as *Prime Movers: The Traits of the Great Wealth Creators* (AMACOM Books, 2000) and *The Essence of Leadership and Goal Setting: A Motivational Technique That Works* (with G. Latham). He is also the editor of *Principles of Organizational Behavior* (Blackwell Publishers, 2000). Dr. Locke is a consulting editor for many professional journals and his commentaries on such topics as animal rights, environmentalism, American values, and education have appeared in the *Los Angeles Times*, *Chicago Tribune*, *Houston Chronicle*, *Dallas Morning News*, *Cincinnati Enquirer*, and the *Boston Globe*.

Arthur Mode, M.D.

Dr. Mode is a psychiatrist in private practice in Falls Church, Virginia, and a senior writer for the Ayn Rand Institute in Marina del Rey, California.

Leonard Peikoff, Ph.D.

Dr. Peikoff is Ayn Rand's legal and intellectual heir, and the leading Objectivist philosopher. He is the author of *Objectivism: The Philosophy of Ayn Rand*, the definitive presentation of Ayn Rand's philosophy. Dr. Peikoff is also the author of *The Ominous Parallels*, which compares the philosophical roots and history of Nazism with similar trends in America. He is editor of several Objectivist anthologies. His commentary has appeared in such newspapers as the *Orange County Register*, *Miami Herald*, *Glendale News-Press*, *Richmond Times-Dispatch*, and the *Los Angeles Times*. From 1995 to 1999, he hosted a nationally syndicated radio talk show, discussing current events from a philosophic perspective. Dr. Peikoff taught philosophy at New York University, Hunter College, the University of Denver, and for many years at the Polytechnic Institute of Brooklyn. He founded the Ayn Rand Institute in 1985.

Richard E. Ralston

Mr. Ralston completed an M.A. in International Relations at the University of Southern California in 1977 after serving seven years in the U.S. Army. He then began a career in newspaper publishing and direct marketing. He has been the circulation director and publisher of *The Christian Science Monitor,* a radio producer, a national television news business manager, and a book publisher. As an independent direct marketing consultant, his clients included IBM, British Airways, CNN, and the *Los Angeles Times*. His book *Communism: Its Rise and Fall in the 20th Century* was published in 1991.

Mr. Ralston was also the editor of the book *Why Businessmen Need Philosophy* (1999). He is now managing director of the Ayn Rand Institute.

Richard M. Salsman

Mr. Salsman is president and chief market strategist of InterMarket Forecasting, which provides quantitative research and forecasts of stocks, bonds, and currencies to guide the asset allocation decisions of institutional investment managers, mutual funds, and pension plans. He is the author of numerous books and articles on economics, banking, and forecasting from a free-market perspective, including *Breaking the Banks: Central Banking Problems and Free Banking Solutions* (American Institute for Economic Research, 1990) and *Gold and Liberty* (American Institute for Economic Research, 1995). Mr. Salsman's work has appeared in *The Intellectual Activist*, the *New York Times, Investor's Business Daily, The Wall Street Journal, Forbes*, and *Barron's*. From 1993 to 1999, he was a senior vice president and senior economist at H.C. Wainwright & Co. Economics. Prior to that he was a banker at Citibank and the Bank of New York. Mr. Salsman is an adjunct fellow at the American Institute for Economic Research and the founder of The Association of Objectivist Businessmen.

Peter Schwartz

Mr. Schwartz is chairman of the board of directors of the Ayn Rand Institute and editorial director of its op-ed program. He was the founding editor and publisher of *The Intellectual Activist*, a periodical covering political, cultural, and philosophic issues. Mr. Schwartz is the author of *The Battle for Laissez-Faire Capitalism*. He is the editor and contributing author of *Return of the Primitive: The Anti-Industrial Revolution* by Ayn Rand (Meridian/Penguin, 1999). He is also president of Second Renaissance Books, a publisher and distributor of pro-reason, pro-individualism titles.

Robert W. Tracinski

Mr. Tracinski is the editor of *The Intellectual Activist*, a magazine analyzing political, cultural, and philosophic issues from an individualist perspective. His commentary has been published in the *San Francisco Chronicle*, *Cincinnati Enquirer*, Los Angeles *Daily News*, *San Jose Mercury News*, and the *Philadelphia Inquirer*. He is the president of the Center for the Moral Defense of Capitalism.

Glenn Woiceshyn

Mr. Woiceshyn is currently home-schooling his grade-five son and a few other grade-five students. He bases his teaching techniques on Ayn Rand's philosophy of Objectivism. Prior to focusing on his son's education, Mr. Woiceshyn was a professional writer. Among his published op-eds was one on school violence that appeared in the *Los Angeles Times*. His op-eds have also appeared in the *Miami Herald*, *Houston Chronicle*, *Philadelphia Inquirer*, *Baltimore Sun*, *Globe and Mail*, and many other newspapers in the United States and Canada. Mr. Woiceshyn received an M.A.Sc. degree in mechanical engineering from the University of Toronto in 1981 and worked thirteen years in the petroleum industry, primarily as a consultant on international projects.

About Ayn Rand

Novelist-philosopher Ayn Rand (1905–1982) embodied the essential characteristics of her fictional heroes. Born in Russia and educated under the Soviets, she rebelled even as a child against the doctrines and practices of that oppressive culture. She finally escaped it, coming to America alone at the age of twenty-one. At the age of nine she had decided to become a writer; in 1936 she published her first novel, *We the Living*, a wrenching portrayal, set in Communist Russia, of the conflict between the individual and the totalitarian state.

The Fountainhead, the story of an architect who refuses to surrender his integrity in the face of overwhelming opposition, was published in 1943—after having been rejected by twelve publishers. It brought Ayn Rand international fame. With the publication of *Atlas Shrugged* in 1957, Ayn Rand's position in history—both as novelist and philosopher—was established. *Atlas Shrugged* tells the story of what happens to the world when its most intelligent and productive members, the men of the mind, go on strike against the socialistic creed of self-immolation.

During the last two decades of her life, Ayn Rand presented her philosophy in nonfiction terms, offering insights and theories on an enormous range of topics, from concept-formation and meta-ethics to the significance of the New Left and to the enjoyment and importance of music. Her most important nonfiction books are *Introduction to Objectivist Epistemology, The Virtue of Selfishness, Capitalism: The Unknown Ideal,* and *The Romantic Manifesto.*

In testament to the power of her ideas, more than twenty million copies of Ayn Rand's books have been sold worldwide; more than 400,000 copies continue to be sold annually. In her book *The Romantic Manifesto,* Ayn Rand identified her fundamental goal and explained her choice of career: "The motive and purpose of my writing can best be summed up by saying that if a dedication page were to precede the total of my work, it would read: To the glory of Man."

About the Ayn Rand Institute

The Ayn Rand Institute (ARI) provides something unique to the best of American business: resounding moral approval.

ARI has published tens of thousands of copies of "The Meaning of Money," an excerpt from Ayn Rand's *Atlas Shrugged*, and distributed them to businessmen—providing a concise, articulate presentation of why money is "the root of all good." Books such as Ayn Rand's *Capitalism: The Unknown Ideal* and *Why Businessmen Need Philosophy* have also been distributed to provide a more in-depth examination of the morality of free markets.

The Institute conducts annual essay contests based on Ayn Rand's *Atlas Shrugged* for graduate and undergraduate business school students. Questions for the contest focus on the moral case for capitalism and free markets. Thousands of dollars in cash prizes are awarded annually for the contest.

Other ARI programs include the Capitalist Self-Defense Project and the publication of editorials in American newspapers—defending the philosophical ideas necessary to build and maintain free markets and a free society.

For additional information and regular updates, we invite you to visit ARI's Web site at www.aynrand.org.